CHURCH

CHURCH

LIVING FAITHFULLY AS THE PEOPLE OF GOD—
COLLECTED INSIGHTS FROM

A. W. TOZER

© 2019 by
THE MOODY BIBLE INSTITUTE
OF CHICAGO

Scripture quotations by A. W. Tozer, unless otherwise indicated, are taken from the King James Version.

All Scripture quotations in epigraphs, unless otherwise indicated, are taken from the Holy Bible, New International Version®, NIV®. Copyright © 1973, 1978, 1984, 2011 by Biblica, Inc.™ Used by permission of Zondervan. All rights reserved worldwide. www.zondervan.com. The "NIV" and "New International Version" are trademarks registered in the United States Patent and Trademark Office by Biblica, Inc.™

Edited by Kevin P. Emmert
Interior and cover design: Erik M. Peterson
Cover art by Aaron Joel Underwood (aaronjoelunderwood.com)

ISBN: 978-0-8024-1828-9

We hope you enjoy this book from Moody Publishers. Our goal is to provide high-quality, thought-provoking books and products that connect truth to your real needs and challenges. For more information on other books and products written and produced from a biblical perspective, go to www.moodypublishers.com or write to:

Moody Publishers
820 N. LaSalle Boulevard
Chicago, IL 60610

1 3 5 7 9 10 8 6 4 2

Printed in the United States of America

CONTENTS

PUBLISHER'S NOTE

As a local church pastor and preacher for much of his life, A. W. Tozer had a passion to see the body of Jesus Christ understand what God has called it to be in the world. He felt that the church in his own day suffered not only from a lack of self-awareness, but also from a lack of commitment to Christ and His commission. Therefore, many of his writings and sermons—which are directed just as much to the church at large as they are to the individual Christian—call the church to awaken from her slumber, to recognize who she is, and to renew her commitment to Christ and His call.

Tozer's message for the church is just as relevant today as it was over half a century ago. Many people today wonder what the church is, whether it has a necessary place in the world, why an individual Christian should be part of a local church, and what the church is called to do. Not only that, many Christians—and also non-Christians—believe the church today is not all that it could be.

The compilation you hold in your hands gathers Tozer's most poignant writings and sermons on the church. It not only details what the church is and does, but also challenges the body of Christ—which is made up of many individual members—to fully embrace its God-given identity and purpose.

Our hope is that this book does more than inform you about one man's ideas about an organization. We pray that this collection gives you a deeper understanding of the church and that you then play your God-given role in it as only you can. God has called you, dear reader, to participate fully in the body of Christ. May this book strengthen and encourage you on your journey.

THE NECESSITY OF THE CHURCH

The church of the living God,
the pillar and foundation of the truth.

1 Timothy 3:15

The highest expression of the will of God in this age is the church, which He purchased with His own blood. To be scripturally valid, any religious activity must be part of the church. Let it be clearly stated that there can be no service acceptable to God in this age that does not center in and spring out of the church. Bible schools, tract societies, Christian businessmen's committees, seminaries, and the many independent groups working at one or another phase of religion need to check themselves reverently and courageously, for they have no true spiritual significance outside of or apart from the church.

According to the Scriptures, the church is the habitation of God through the Spirit, and as such is the most important organism beneath the sun. She is not one more good institution along with the home, the state, and the school; she is the most vital of all institutions—the only one that can claim a heavenly origin.

The cynic may inquire which church we mean, and may remind us that the Christian church is so divided that it is impossible to tell which is the true one, even if such a one exists. But we are not too much troubled by the suppressed smile of the doubter. Being inside the church, we are probably as well aware of her faults as any person on the outside could possibly be. And we believe in her nevertheless, wherever she manifests herself in a world of darkness and unbelief.

The church is found wherever the Holy Spirit has drawn together a few persons who trust Christ for their salvation, worship God in spirit, and have no dealings with the world and the flesh. The members may, by necessity, be scattered over the surface of the earth and separated by distance and circumstances, but in every true member of the church is the homing instinct and the longing of the sheep for the fold and the shepherd. Give a few real Christians half a chance, and they will get together and organize and plan regular meetings for prayer and worship. In these meetings, they will hear the Scriptures expounded, break bread together in one form or another according to their light, and try as far as possible to spread the saving gospel to the lost world.

Such groups are cells in the body of Christ, and each one is a true church, a real part of the greater church. It is in and through these cells that the Spirit does His work on earth. Whoever scorns the local church scorns the body of Christ.

The church is still to be reckoned with. "The gates of hell shall not prevail against it" (Matt. 16:18).

2

THE LORD
OF THE CHURCH

*All authority in heaven
and on earth has been given to me.*

MATTHEW 28:18

Jesus Christ has today almost no authority at all among the groups that call themselves by His name. By these I mean not the Roman Catholics nor the liberals, nor the various quasi-Christian cults. I do mean Protestant churches generally, and I include those that protest the loudest that they are in spiritual descent from our Lord and His apostles—namely, the evangelicals.

It is a basic doctrine of the New Testament that after His resurrection the man Jesus was declared by God to be both Lord and Christ, and that He was invested by the Father with absolute Lordship over the church, which is His body. All authority is His in heaven and in earth. In His own proper time, He will exert it to the full, but during this period in history, He allows this authority to be challenged or ignored. And just now it is being challenged by the world and ignored by the church.

A LORD UNRECOGNIZED

The present position of Christ in the gospel churches may be likened to that of a king in a limited, constitutional monarchy. The king (sometimes depersonalized by the term "the Crown") is in such a country no more than a traditional rallying point, a pleasant symbol of unity and loyalty much like a flag or a national anthem. He is lauded, feted, and supported, but his real authority is small. Nominally, he is head over all, but in every crisis someone else makes the decisions. On formal occasions he appears in his royal attire to deliver the tame, colorless speech put into his mouth by the real rulers of the country. The whole thing may be no more than good-natured make-believe, but it is rooted in antiquity, it is a lot of fun and no one wants to give it up.

Among the gospel churches, Christ is now in fact little more than a beloved symbol. "All Hail the Power of Jesus' Name" is the church's national anthem and the cross is her official flag, but in the week-by-week services of the church and the day-by-day conduct of her members someone else, not Christ, makes the decisions. Under proper circumstances, Christ is allowed to say, "Come unto me, all ye that labour and are heavy laden" or "Let not your heart be troubled," but when the speech is finished, someone else takes over. Those in actual authority decide the moral standards of the church, as well as all objectives and all methods employed to achieve them. Because of long and meticulous organization, it is now possible for the youngest pastor just out of seminary to have more actual authority in a church than Jesus Christ has.

Not only does Christ have little or no authority, His influence also is becoming less and less. I would not say that He has none, only that it is small and diminishing. A fair parallel would be the influence of Abraham Lincoln over the American people. Honest Abe is still the idol of the country. The likeness of his kind, rugged face, so homely that it is beautiful, appears everywhere. It is easy to grow misty-eyed over him. Children are brought up on stories of his love, his honesty, and his humility.

But after we have gotten control over our tender emotions what have we left? No more than a good example that, as it recedes into the past, becomes more and more unreal and exercises less and less real influence. Every scoundrel is ready to wrap Lincoln's long, black coat around him. In the cold light of political facts in the United States, the constant appeal to Lincoln by the politicians is a cynical joke.

The Lordship of Jesus is not quite forgotten among Christians, but it has been relegated to the hymnal, where all responsibility toward it may be comfortably discharged in a glow of pleasant religious emotion. Or if it is taught as a theory in the classroom, it is rarely applied to practical living. The idea that the Man Christ Jesus has absolute and final authority over the whole church and over all of its members in every detail of their lives is simply not now accepted as true by the rank and file of evangelical Christians.

What we do is this: we accept the Christianity of our group as being identical with that of Christ and His apostles. The beliefs, the practices, the ethics, the activities of our group are equated with the Christianity of the New Testament. Whatever the group thinks or says or does is scriptural, no questions asked. It is assumed that all our Lord expects of us is that we busy ourselves with the activities of the group. In so doing, we are keeping the commandments of Christ.

To avoid the hard necessity of either obeying or rejecting the plain instructions of our Lord in the New Testament, we take refuge in a liberal interpretation of them. Casuistry is not the possession of Roman Catholic theologians alone. We evangelicals also know how to avoid the sharp point of obedience by means of fine and intricate explanations. These are tailor-made for the flesh. They excuse disobedience, comfort carnality, and make the words of Christ of none effect. And the essence of it all is that Christ simply could not have meant what He said. His teachings are accepted even theoretically only after they have been weakened by interpretation.

Yet Christ is consulted by increasing numbers of persons with "problems" and sought after by those who long for peace of mind. He is widely recommended as a kind of spiritual psychiatrist with remarkable powers to straighten people out. He is able to deliver them from their guilt complexes and to help them to avoid serious psychic traumas by making a smooth and easy adjustment to society and to their own ids. Of course this strange Christ has no relation whatever to the Christ of the New Testament. The true Christ is also Lord, but this accommodating Christ is little more than the servant of the people.

A LORD UNCONSULTED

I suppose I should offer some concrete proof to support my charge that Christ has little or no authority today among the churches. Well, let me put a few questions and let the answers be the evidence.

What church board consults our Lord's words to decide matters under discussion? Let anyone reading this who has had experience on a church board try to recall the times or time when any board member read from the Scriptures to make a point, or when any chairman suggested that the brethren should see what instructions the Lord had for them on a particular question. Board meetings are habitually opened with a formal prayer or "a season of prayer." After that the Head of the church is respectfully silent while the "real" rulers take over. Let anyone who denies this bring forth evidence to refute it. I for one will be glad to hear it.

What Sunday school committee goes to the Word for directions? Do not the members invariably assume that they already know what they are supposed to do and that their only problem is to find effective means to get it done? Plans, rules, "operations," and new methodological techniques absorb all their time and attention. The prayer before the meeting is for divine help to carry out their plans. Apparently the idea that the Lord might have some instructions for them never so much as enters their heads.

Who remembers when a conference chairman brought his Bible to the table with him for the purpose of using it? Minutes, regulations, rules of order, yes. The sacred commandments of the Lord, no. An absolute dichotomy exists between the devotional period and the business session. The first has no relation to the second.

What foreign mission board actually seeks to follow the guidance of the Lord as provided by His Word and His Spirit? They all think they do, but what they do in fact is to assume the scripturalness of their ends and then ask for help to find ways to achieve them. They may pray all night for God to give success to their enterprises, but Christ is desired as their helper, not as their Lord. Human means are devised to achieve ends assumed to be divine. These harden into policy, and thereafter the Lord doesn't even have a vote.

In the conduct of our public worship, where is the authority of Christ to be found? The truth is that today the Lord rarely controls a service, and the influence He exerts is very small. We sing of Him and preach about Him, but He must not interfere; we worship our way, and it must be right because we have always done it that way, as have the other churches in our group.

What Christian, when faced with a moral problem, goes straight to the Sermon on the Mount or other New Testament Scripture for the authoritative answer? Who lets the words of Christ be final on giving, birth control, the bringing up of a family, personal habits, tithing, entertainment, buying, selling, and other such important matters?

What theological school, from the lowly Bible institute up, could continue to operate if it were to make Christ Lord of its every policy? There may be some, and I hope there are, but I believe I am right when I say that most such schools, to stay in business, are forced to adopt procedures that find no justification in the Bible they profess to teach. So we have this strange anomaly: the authority of Christ is ignored in order to maintain a school to teach, among other things, the authority of Christ.

TWO LORDS OF THE CHURCH

The causes of the decline in our Lord's authority are many. I name only two.

One is the power of custom, precedent, and tradition within the older religious groups. These, like gravitation, affect every particle of religious practice within the group, exerting a steady and constant pressure in one direction. Of course that direction is toward conformity to the status quo. Not Christ but custom is lord in this situation. And the same thing has passed over (possibly to a slightly lesser degree) into the other groups such as the full gospel tabernacles, the holiness churches, the Pentecostal and fundamental churches, and the many independent and undenominational churches found everywhere throughout the North American continent.

The second cause is the revival of intellectualism among the evangelicals. This, if I sense the situation correctly, is not so much a thirst for learning as a desire for a reputation of being learned. Because of it, good men who ought to know better are being put in the position of collaborating with the enemy. I'll explain.

Our evangelical faith—which I believe to be the true faith of Christ and His apostles—is being attacked these days from many different directions. In the Western world, the enemy has forsworn violence. He comes against us no more with sword and [missile]; he now comes smiling, bearing gifts. He raises his eyes to heaven and swears that he too believes in the faith of our fathers, but his real purpose is to destroy that faith, or at least to modify it to such an extent that it is no longer the supernatural thing it once was. He comes in the name of philosophy or psychology or anthropology, and with sweet reasonableness urges us to rethink our historic position, to be less rigid, more tolerant, more broadly understanding.

He speaks in the sacred jargon of the schools, and many of our half-educated evangelicals run to fawn on him. He tosses academic degrees to the scrambling sons of the prophets as Rockefeller used to toss dimes to the children of the peasants. The evangelicals who, with some justification, have been accused of lacking true scholarship, now grab for these status symbols with shining eyes, and when they get them they are scarcely able to believe their eyes. They walk about in a kind of ecstatic unbelief, much as the soloist of the neighborhood church choir might were she to be invited to sing at La Scala.

IS CHRIST YOUR LORD?

For the true Christian, the one supreme test for the present soundness and ultimate worth of everything religious must be the place our Lord occupies in it. Is He Lord or symbol? Is He in charge of the project or merely one of the crew? Does He decide things or only help to carry out the plans of others? All religious activities, from the simplest act of an individual Christian to the ponderous and expensive operations of a whole denomination, may be proved by the answer to the question, "Is Jesus Christ Lord in this act?" Whether our works prove to be wood, hay, and stubble or gold and silver and precious stones in that great day will depend upon the right answer to that question.

What, then, are we to do? Each one of us must decide, and there are at least three possible choices. One is to rise up in shocked indignation and accuse me of irresponsible reporting. Another is to nod general agreement with what is written here but take comfort in the fact that there are exceptions and we are among the exceptions. The other is to go down in meek humility and confess that we have grieved the Spirit and dishonored our Lord in failing to give Him the place His Father has given Him as Head and Lord of the church.

Either the first or the second will but confirm the wrong. The third if carried out to its conclusion can remove the curse. The decision lies with us.

THE SPIRIT
OF THE CHURCH

*You will receive power when
the Holy Spirit comes on you.*

ACTS 1:8

S ome good Christians have misread this text and have assumed that Christ told his disciples that they were to receive
the Holy Spirit *and* power, the power to come after the coming
of the Spirit. A superficial reading of the King James text might
conceivably lead to that conclusion, but the truth is that Christ
taught not the coming of the Holy Spirit *and* power, but the
coming of the Holy Spirit *as* power; the power and the Spirit are
the same.

Our mother tongue is a beautiful and facile instrument, but
it can also be a tricky and misleading one, and for this reason it
must be used with care if we would avoid giving and receiving
wrong impressions by its means. Especially is this true when we
are speaking of God, for God being wholly unlike anything or

anybody in His universe, our very thoughts of Him as well as our words are in constant danger of going astray. One example is found in the words, "The power of God." The danger is that we think of "power" as something belonging to God as muscular energy belongs to a man, as something that He *has* and that might be separated from Him and still have existence in itself. We must remember that the attributes of God are not component parts of the blessed Godhead nor elements out of which He is composed. A god who could be *composed* would not be God at all but the work of something or someone greater than he, great enough to compose him. We would then have a synthetic god made out of the pieces we call attributes, and the true God would be another Being altogether, One indeed who is above all thought and all conceiving.

The Bible and Christian theology teach that God is an indivisible Unity, being what He is in undivided oneness, from whom nothing can be taken and to whom nothing can be added. Mercy, for instance, immutability, eternity, these are but names that we have given to something that God has declared to be true of Himself. All the "of God" expressions in the Bible must be understood to mean not what God has but *what God is* in His undivided and indivisible Unity. Even the word "nature" when applied to God should be understood as an accommodation to our human way of looking at things and not as an accurate description of anything true of the mysterious Godhead. God has said, "I AM THAT I AM," and we can only repeat in reverence, "O God, Thou art."

Our Lord before His ascension said to His disciples, "Tarry ye in the city of Jerusalem, until ye be endued with power from on high" (Luke 24:49). That word *until* is a time-word; it indicates a point in relation to which everything is either before or after. So the experience of those disciples could be stated like this: up to that point they *had not* received the power; at that point they *did* receive the power; after that point they *had* received the power. Such is the plain historic fact. Power came upon the church, such power as had never been released into human nature before (with the lone exception of that mighty anointing that came upon Christ at the waters of Jordan). That power, still active in the church, has enabled her to exist for nearly twenty centuries, even though for all of that time she has remained a highly unpopular minority group among the nations of mankind and has always been surrounded by enemies who would gladly have ended her existence if they could have done so.

"Ye shall receive power" (Acts 1:8). By those words our Lord raised the expectation of His disciples and taught them to look forward to the coming of a supernatural potency into their natures from a source outside of themselves. It was to be something previously unknown to them, but suddenly to come upon them from another world. It was to be nothing less than God himself entering into them with the purpose of ultimately reproducing His own likeness within them.

Here is the dividing line that separates Christianity from all occultism and from every kind of oriental cult, ancient or modern. These are all built around the same ideas, varying only in minor details, each with its own peculiar set of phrases and apparently vying with each other in vagueness and obscurity. They each advise, "Get in tune with the Infinite," or "Wake the giant within you," or "Tune in to your hidden potentialities," or

"Learn to think creatively." All this may have some fleeting value as a psychological shot in the arm, but its results are not permanent because at its best it builds its hopes upon the fallen nature of man and knows no invasion from above. And whatever may be said in its favor, *it most certainly is not Christianity*. ✓

Christianity takes for granted the absence of any self-help and offers a power that is nothing less than the power of God. This power is to come upon powerless men as a gentle but resistless invasion from another world bringing a moral potency infinitely beyond anything that might be stirred up from within. This power is sufficient; no additional help is needed, no auxiliary source of spiritual energy, for it is the Holy Spirit of God come where the weakness lay to supply power and grace to meet the moral need.

Set over against such a mighty provision as this ethical Christianity (if I may be allowed the term) is seen to be no Christianity at all. An infantile copying of Christ's "ideals," a pitiable effort to carry out the teachings of the Sermon on the Mount! All this is but religious child's play and is not the faith of Christ and the New Testament.

"Ye shall receive power." This was and is a unique afflatus, an enduement of supernatural energy affecting every department of the believer's life and remaining with him forever. It is not physical power nor even mental power, though it may touch everything both mental and physical in its benign outworkings. It is too another kind of power than that seen in nature, in the lunar attraction that creates the tides or the angry flash that splits the great oak during a storm. This power from God operates on another level and affects another department of His wide creation.

It is spiritual power. It is the kind of power that God is. It is the ability to achieve spiritual and moral ends. Its long-range result is to produce Godlike character in men and women who were once wholly evil by nature and by choice.

Now how does this power operate? At its purest, it is an unmediated force directly applied by the Spirit of God to the spirit of man. The wrestler achieves his ends by the pressure of his physical body upon the body of his opponent, the teacher by the pressure of ideas upon the mind of the student, the moralist by the pressure of duty upon the conscience of the disciple. So the Holy Spirit performs His blessed work by direct contact with the human spirit.

It would be less than accurate to say that the power of God is always experienced in a direct and unmediated form, for when He so wills, the Spirit may use other means, as Christ used spittle to heal a blind man. But always the power is above and beyond the means. While the Spirit may use appropriate means to bless a believing man, He never need do so for they are at best but temporary concessions made to our ignorance and unbelief. Where adequate power is present, almost any means will suffice, but where the power is absent, not all the means in the world can secure the desired end. The Spirit of God may use a song, a sermon, a good deed, a text, or the mystery and majesty of nature, but always the final work will be done by the pressure of the inliving Spirit upon the human heart.

In the light of this it will be seen how empty and meaningless is the average church service today. All the means are in evidence; the one ominous weakness is the absence of the Spirit's power. The form of godliness is there, and often the form is perfected till it is an aesthetic triumph. Music and poetry, art and oratory, symbolic vesture and solemn tones combine to charm the mind of the worshiper, but too often the supernatural afflatus is not there. The power from on high is neither known nor desired by pastor or people. This is nothing less than tragic, and all the more so because it falls within the field of religion where the eternal destinies of men are involved.

To the absence of the Spirit may be traced that vague sense of unreality that almost everywhere invests religion in our times. In the average church service, the most real thing is the shadowy unreality of everything. The worshiper sits in a state of suspended mentation; a kind of dreamy numbness creeps upon him; he hears words, but they do not register; he cannot relate them to anything on his own life-level. He is conscious of having entered a kind of half-world; his mind surrenders itself to a more or less pleasant mood that passes with the benediction, leaving no trace behind. It does not affect anything in his everyday life. He is aware of no power, no presence, no spiritual reality. There is simply nothing in his experience corresponding to the things that he heard from the pulpit or sang in the hymns.

One meaning of the word "power" is "ability to do." There precisely is the wonder of the Spirit's work in the church and in the hearts of Christians, His sure ability to make spiritual things real to the soul. This power can go straight to its object with piercing directness; it can diffuse itself through the mind like an infinitely fine volatile essence, securing ends above and beyond the limits of the intellect. Reality is its subject matter, reality in heaven and upon earth. It does not create objects that are not there but reveals objects already present and hidden from the soul. In actual human experience, this is likely to be the first felt in a heightened sense of the presence of Christ. He is felt to be a real Person and to be intimately, ravishingly near. Then all other spiritual objects begin to stand out clearly before the mind. Grace, forgiveness, cleansing take on a form of almost bodily clearness. Prayer loses its unmeaning quality and becomes a sweet conversation with Someone actually there. Love for God and for the children of God takes possession of the soul. We feel ourselves near to heaven and it is now the earth and the world that begin to seem unreal. We know them now for what they are, realities indeed, but like stage scenery, here for one brief hour and soon to pass away. The world to come takes on a hard outline before our minds and begins to invite our interest and our devotion. Then the whole life changes to suit the new reality, and the change is permanent. Slight fluctuations there may be like the rise and dip of the line on a graph, but the established direction is upward, and the ground taken is held.

This is not all, but it will give a fair idea of what is meant when the New Testament speaks of *power*, and perhaps by contrast, we may learn how little of the power we enjoy.

I think there can be no doubt that the need above all other needs in the church of God at this moment is the power of the Holy Spirit. More education, better organization, finer equipment, more advanced methods—all are unavailing. It is like bringing a better pulmotor after the patient is dead. Good as these things are, they can never give life. "It is the spirit that quickeneth" (John 6:63). Good as they are, they can never bring power. "Power belongeth unto God" (Ps. 62:11). Protestantism is on the wrong road when it tries to win merely by means of a "united front." It is not organizational unity we need most; the great need is power. The headstones in the cemetery present a united front, but they stand mute and helpless while the world passes by.

I suppose my suggestion will not receive much serious attention, but I should like to suggest that we Bible-believing Christians announce a moratorium on religious activity and set our house in order preparatory to the coming of an afflatus from above. So carnal is the body of Christians that composes the conservative wing of the church, so shockingly irreverent are our public services in some quarters, so degraded are our religious tastes in still others, that the need for power could scarcely have been greater at any time in history. I believe we should profit immensely were we to declare a period of silence and self-examination during which each one of us searched his own heart and sought to meet every condition for a real baptism of power from on high.

We may be sure of one thing, that for our deep trouble there is no cure apart from a visitation, yes, an *invasion* of power from above. Only the Spirit Himself can show us what is wrong with us, and only the Spirit can prescribe the cure. Only the Spirit can save us from the numbing unreality of Spiritless Christianity. Only the Spirit can show us the Father and the Son. Only the in-working of the Spirit's power can discover to us the solemn majesty and the heart-ravishing mystery of the Triune God.

THE ORGANIZATION OF THE CHURCH

The reason I left you in Crete was that
you might put in order what was left unfinished.

TITUS 1:5

Crete was inhabited by a rather loud mixture of races, religions, and philosophies. There were a lot of Jews there, and it was supposed to be the birthplace of Bacchus. You've heard the word *bacchanalian*, meaning wild, drunken orgies. And that was the kind of religion they had there. Old Bacchus, they said, was born on that island Crete. And their religion sort of centered around Bacchus. And, of course, there was drunkenness and all kinds of immoralities that went with the religion they had. Then there were Jews who held rather closely to the Jewish religion.

Then when the Christians came, of course, they pulled loose, both from the orgies of the Bacchanalian worshipers who worship false gods and from the Jews.

There was a large number of Christians on Crete when Paul

got there. Titus and Paul were traveling together, just as two preachers or two missionaries might start out together, or just like a man and his wife might start out somewhere. And when Paul saw the situation in Crete, he left his young friend there and said, "Now, Titus, I haven't time to stay here and organize, but this place is a mess. You have to stay here and organize."

I don't know what the slang word was for what was wrong with them there. Dr. R. Brown says it's *status quo*. The preacher kept referring to the *status quo* in the church, and somebody asked what that meant, and he said it was Latin for "the mess we were in." The *status quo* in Crete among the Christians was very bad. And Paul said, "You stay, Titus, and I'll go on. You stay and set it in order." There was, said somebody, plenty of Christian life but no Christian organization.

THE NEED FOR ORGANIZATION

Now some persons despise organization, and they quote this passage: "where two are three are gathered together in my name, there am I in the midst of them" (Matt. 18:20). And they say, "Now there, you have your church, that's your typical church. And all churches should take that for a standard: a few people gathered together in the name of Christ." Well they are right that far. But have you noticed that their idea is no authority, no order, no form, no obedience—just freedom, and fellowship, and equality, and joy? It is a sort of ideal state that they think up but never has been realized. ✓

The Scriptures teach quite otherwise. The Scriptures teach not that a church consists of a group of people, two or three or more, met together, without order, organization, obedience, and authority. The Bible teaches something else altogether.

Now, Israel was organized thoroughly. If you read your Old Testament, you will see that nothing was left to people. God organized Israel from the top, and He organized it clear down to the last Kohathite to carry on his shoulder the accoutrements of the temple. And then those first disciples that gathered around Jesus had some kind of organization because they did have a treasurer.

They say that if there were three Americans on a desert island, one would take a stick and call the other two to order, and they would have a meeting. And they would elect a president, a vice-president, and a secretary—and if there were four, a treasurer. But you find that Judas was the treasurer. He turned out bad, but he was tempted more than the others were, and he probably wasn't ever a born-again man. So, he turned out bad. But they did have a treasurer. Somebody kept the bag.

Then Acts 6—did you notice what happens when it ceases to be two or three and it becomes more? "And in those days, when the number of the disciples was multiplied, there arose a murmuring of the Grecians against the Hebrews." The Grecian Christians were Jewish proselytes, I understand, and were from other countries and were in Jerusalem. Then there were the Christian Hebrews, blown in the bottle, real Hebrews that were Hebrews of the land. They spoke one language, and the Grecians might have spoken almost anything. From whatever land they came, they would speak that language. But they were all Christians. And the disciples multiplied, and there arose a murmur. "Then the twelve called the multitude of the disciples unto them," not two or three, but the multitude.

31

See the problem came from numbers. Always remember that. Lots of people want a tiny, little church with only a few. They say, "Oh, it's so much better." But always remember the proverb that says, "Where no oxen are, the crib is clean: but much increase is by the strength of the ox" (Prov. 14:4). What does that mean? It means if you just want a clean barn, don't have any oxen. But if you want your farm to grow, and you want to have much fruit and much increase, you are going to have to have oxen. And if you are going to have to have oxen, you are going to have to keep cleaning out the stables and looking after the oxen. If all you want is a nice, clean barn, why, you will have no fruit, no vegetables, no grain. And otherwise it has been said, "You can't make an omelet without breaking an egg."

If you are going to reach a lot of people, you are going to have to take the problem of having more people. So the early church had to face it out. "Then the twelve called the multitude of the disciples unto them, and said, It is not reason that we should leave the word of God, and serve tables. Wherefore, brethren, look ye out among you seven men of honest report, full of the Holy Ghost and wisdom, whom we may appoint over this business" (Acts 6:2–3). They said, "Pick them out; you know them better than we do, find the best people possible, and we'll appoint them. But we will give ourselves continually to prayer and to the ministry of the word" (see Acts 6:3–4).

They picked out seven of them, and it names them. "Whom they set before the apostles: and when they had prayed, they laid their hands on them" (Acts 6:6).

There was organization in the sixth chapter of Acts. As long as there were two or three gathered together in the name of the Lord, there would be no reason for organization. But as soon as the multitude or the number of the disciples increased, then there had to come some sort of organization.

GOD'S ORDER

The Pastoral Epistles—Titus and 1 and 2 Timothy—deal with organization, order, obedience, and authority in the church. And then 1 Peter 5 says, "The elders which are among you I exhort. . . . Feed the flock of God which is among you, taking the oversight thereof, not by constraint, but willingly; not for filthy lucre, but of a ready mind; neither as being lords over God's heritage, but being examples to the flock" (vv. 1–3). And Paul says, "Thou shouldest . . . ordain elders in every city, as I had appointed thee" (Titus 1:5).

Now I want to ask a question, if these elders were selected by the congregation, approved by Titus, and appointed by the apostle, then I wonder, where is all that democracy we hear so much about? Go back through the Old Testament, and you find that when the Lord wanted to lead the children of Israel out of Egypt, He selected one man, and He worked through that man. And when He wanted to lead them into the Promised Land, He selected another man. When He wanted to lead them back from Babylon, He selected two men. And all down throughout the years it has been the same.

It seems to be inherent in crowds that they can't hear God speak. A man has to get alone and pay the price for listening, and then when He hears God speak, He goes to the people and tells them, and they hear God speak through him. That seems to be the order, the biblical order, and I'll stand up to anybody on that. That is why I can't go along with my good friends the Plymouth Brethren. I admire them, I learn from them. Yet I can't go along with them on their refusal to acknowledge pastors and so on. Now here was the order: Paul at the top, Titus beneath him, the elders still further down on the totem pole. That seems to be God's order.

Now, what do I gather from all this? Well, I'm a good fundamentalist. I'll give you seven points, just briefly, that I learned from Paul, who said, "left I thee in Crete, that thou shouldest set in order the things that are wanting, and ordain elders . . . as I had appointed thee." Here's what I gather from this, these seven points.

1. Wherever there is corporate action, there must be organization. Otherwise there can be no order, and where there is no order, there can only be chaos and wasted motion. Any group of Christians meeting together—if they are going to function as a church, as a body of Christ, they've got to have some sort of organization. The great proof of this lies in 1 Corinthians 12, where Paul likens the church to the body. And a body is organized. If it isn't organized, then you will have dear poor people.

I have a friend. He is one of the most learned fellows I have ever known. He teaches Advanced Greek in college, but he can't control himself. He's a spastic. He simply goes all to pieces. He has to be fed. He has to have his clothes put on him. He can hardly hold a book. He is just all over the place. He can't even control his face. He smiles, but his smile goes all awry. He's a brilliant fellow. I have watched him now for the last fifteen years or more, growing. He sits before a class, and he teaches brilliantly. But he is a spastic.

Well, a body that isn't organized is like that. It would go all to pieces. It has to be organized. Your brain has to tell your nerves what to tell your muscles, and your muscles have to have the cooperation of the joints, and the whole thing has to work together. So the church of Christ must be. If it is going to work, it is going to have to be organized. Our problem comes when we organize after they are dead. I find that more organization is usually an indication of lack of spirituality. A certain amount of organization is necessary to control life. But when life goes out, then we try to make up by organization what we lack in life. That happens in churches.

2. To be a true New Testament church, there must be offices, authority, and obedience. If we are not ready and willing as Christians to admit this, then we are going to have to walk right out of the New Testament, because that is what it teaches.

3. Organization is a New Testament doctrine. You know, good men can say things that they never should have said. Someone once asked Charles Haddon Spurgeon, "Mr. Spurgeon, have you ever been ordained?" He gave this classic reply: "No," he said. "Nobody has ever laid his empty hands on my empty head."* And that was quoted all over the world. Moody said something about the same, and he never was ordained. The result was that layman-ism took over. And we see it today in its

---

* Spurgeon is quoted elsewhere saying, "Empty hands, it seems to me, are fitly laid on empty heads," in *The Metropolitan Tabernacle Pulpit: Sermons Preached and Revised by C. H. Spurgeon During the Year 1872*, vol. 18 (London: Passmore & Alabaster, 1873), 626.

crassness and rawness throughout the whole evangelical church.

But in spite of a quip some fellow might make in a weak moment, ordination is a New Testament doctrine. And so whoever rejects that also rejects the Scripture, because Scripture very clearly teaches it: "Look ye out among you seven men of honest report" (Acts 6:3). They know who they were, but they didn't function until the apostles laid their hands on them and prayed for them and ordained them to their specific ministry.

4. God gives no man dictatorial authority over a church. He gives him a position, and He gives him a certain spiritual authority that the church, if it is a church of God, will recognize. But He gives him no right to call all the shots and to rule everybody's life and to stand up and dictate. Peter says, "Neither as being lords over God's heritage, but being examples to the flock" (1 Peter 5:3). They are to be shepherds to lead the flock, not sergeants to command the flock. There is a difference there. And good leaders are those who lead us, not those who command us.

5. The pastor is not a hired man. That ought to be remembered also by churches. There are boards, and I never was unfortunate enough to ever have to deal with any of them. They imagine that the pastor is a hired man. I remember in Canada there was a church, one of our great Alliance churches, and they had there one of the senators, I believe, or a member of parliament anyways. He was a member of the church. And they had a military officer who was in charge of the orchestra. So they invited a pastor to come, and the pastor wanted to know who was chairman of the board. They said, "That is not any of your responsibility, Reverend. You come and preach, and we will run the church." In other words, "You are a hired man. And we hire you to come and we'll run the church." No, that is not the way it is. The pastor is not a hired man. Neither is he a dictator. He is one of the crowd, ordained by God to take a certain leadership, and the flock follows him as he follows the Lord. But never think of him as a hired man to be hired and fired at the dictation of some board member who had a bad day at the office and who, when he came to the meeting, wasn't feeling well.

6. Too much democracy is bad for religion. We desperately need the right kind of leadership now. We need it in the church. We are getting a certain kind of leadership. But it is not the leadership of the Holy Ghost. It is a lay leadership in the direction of all sorts of organizations, all sorts of new schemes and methodology as they say. And the result is that we have democratized ourselves to death. Nobody is willing to stand out and lead. We want men who will go along with the crowd.

7. The right order is: gifts and offices and democracy and cooperation. That is the right order. Gifts in the church that are recognized by the people. Then those gifted men are ordained to offices in the church. Then democracy, meaning that the people, God's sheep, have a voice. They have a say, and they help to select those that are to set things in order. But they do not finally select the men. No one becomes an elder by election. Keep that in mind. He can become an elder only by ordination. And if the great God Almighty doesn't ordain a man, he is not an elder, no matter how often he may be elected.

Democracy? Yes, there is some democracy in the church. Pure democracy? No. Leadership? Yes. Dictatorship? No. Fellowship? Yes. Cooperation? Certainly. Order? Absolutely. Organization? There must be. All that is implied here in Titus. The rest of Titus, the two Timothys, 1 Corinthians, and the book of Acts all bear out what I just discussed. But it is wonderful to work together, to have everybody doing his job and operating—nobody angry, nobody mad, nobody jealous, everybody willing to do their job, not by constraint, but willingly.

THE LEADERSHIP OF THE CHURCH

The reason I left you in Crete was that you might put in order what was left unfinished and appoint elders in every town, as I directed you.

TITUS 1:5

This is authoritative and inspired, the language of an apostle. And he says to the man Titus, "For this cause left I thee in Crete, that thou shouldest set in order the things that are wanting, and ordain elders in every city, as I had appointed thee."

Now he said, "Ordain elders in every city, as I had appointed thee." And then he said, "If any be blameless." Then in verse 7 he says, "For a bishop must be blameless, as the steward of God." Now blamelessness here is not a virtue. Blamelessness is a summation of the other virtues. See he didn't say, "Be blameless, be good, be hospitable, be clean." He said, "Be blameless, and here is what I mean by blameless." That was Paul's method, and here we see it laid out before us. And he said, "Ordain elders

. . . for a bishop must be blameless." We ought to talk a little bit about this, I suppose. If I wanted to follow the usual method of Bible teaching, I could shift you back and forth from one New Testament book to another, from 1 Timothy, 2 Timothy, Titus and back again and shift back and forth. But I don't intend to do it because the people to whom Paul wrote didn't have those other books. And Paul, I suppose, assumed he had enough to say here in Titus that they wouldn't have to refer to other books. So I am not going to refer to them, but try to stick close to this one book.

TYPES OF LEADERS

We have the word *elder* and the word *bishop* mentioned here. Now we are living hundreds of years from the beginning of the New Testament church. And much water has gone over the dam, and many people have risen with strong opinions, and many strong dictatorial minds have impressed themselves upon the church during the centuries. And this bishop, elder, and deacons deal has been more or less impressed upon the churches. You think they get these ideas from the Bible. But actually, the New Testament is not very clear about all of this. It lays down the principles but leaves the outworking of them to the church. And the result is that we have very strong divisions in the church. Not so much divisions as differing views. For instance, the word *bishop* here is the word from which we get our Episcopal ideas: the form of government known as Episcopal, with bishops and arch-bishops; it's a kind of autocratic rule from the top by the bishops. And then the Presbyterian form of government comes from what is called the presbyter; that's from the word *elder*.

Paul uses both of them and uses them synonymously. That's a strange thing, that *bishop* and *elder* in the mind of Paul were the same person. An elder was the title, and a bishop outlined his duties. So when you hear Paul say, "I told you to ordain elders, for a bishop must be blameless," he is not contradicting himself, and the translators were not off. There were two different words there. One meant "elder"—simply, what it means now, an older person. And that was Jewish, or at least the idea came from the Jews. The older men were picked, seventy of them. They were the Sanhedrin. They were the leaders, older men. No young men got in there because they didn't have experience. Only the older men. So the church picked this up—the word *elder*, to mean "an older person." But there is no age set. Some people are as old at forty as they are at ninety. Some never do get old, and some are never young. But the thought is simply that a little more time will give you opportunity to be a little wiser, a little broader-minded.

So the church picked elders. That is describing the man as an older, honored brother. But his duty is summed up under the word *bishop*, and that was born from the Roman form of government. And it meant "an inspector, an overseer, a ruler."

Certain churches will not use the word *reverend*; they use the word *elder*. Other churches use the word *overseer*. As a Christian, you ought to be big enough to take in all the good that they can give you, but be bigger than all of it. Those who take the word *bishop* and then form the Episcopal form of government out of it—we won't condemn them, and we will thank God for all of them. And you can hardly go through a service without singing a hymn by some Episcopal bishop. So it is alright. Or, over on the other side there is the Presbyterian form of government ruled by elders. You're not going to complain about that because you can hardly pick up a devotional book or sing a hymn without finding a Presbyterian in it. Of course, the Methodists were Episcopal in their form of government, and for years were known as the Methodist-Episcopal church. Now they are simply called the Methodist church. The "Episcopal" referred to their form of government, so that an elder and a bishop in the Scripture seemed to be about the same thing. I wondered if I might not be extreme on this. In my study, I checked the famous *Smith's Bible Dictionary*. And they say the same thing; you have two different words to mean about the same office. It is an office of some authority. But it is not the final authority the Episcopals give it.

Then there is the word *deacon*. Deacons were supposed to be young men and we're not so far as I know dealing with it here. *Deacon* is not synonymous with *bishop* or *elder*. They were the ones who did the work around the church. That is, they served tables and all that sort of thing. You remember Ananias and Sapphira when they died? Remember who carried them out? The deacons, the young men, carried them out. That is in Acts 5. Then in chapter 6, those young men were ordained, hands were laid on them, and they became officially deacons in the church.

But there are other officers. There is that of the apostle. Then there is the gift of the pastor, and the gifts that we have talked about in great length as time has gone by.

QUALITIES OF A LEADER

Now to be blameless as God's steward—about whom are we speaking then? Well, we are speaking about anybody who holds an office in a church. And if it is true of them, then it certainly ought to be true of every one of God's children. God has no double standard. He does not say, "Now, you saints are supposed to be very, very pure," and from the saints we draw our priesthood. No, God wants all of His people to be holy, and anything said here about an elder also should apply to the newest convert, or as soon as he can develop and grow in spirituality, at least the standard is there for him.

Now, blameless is God's steward. A man hasn't anything to give. He is a dispenser of God's work. He is God's steward, and he is to be blameless. Now I might say that it doesn't say "faultless." There has been no faultless person that has ever lived. I think Adam was the only faultless man, and he couldn't have been faultless or he wouldn't have fallen.

But faultlessness is not to be looked for. For instance, take a man like Johnathon Edwards. He wasn't a faultless man. He was a man who made mistakes. Though he was probably the greatest evangelist, second to Finny, that ever touched the American shores, he nevertheless made so many blunders that they actually threw him out of his church on one occasion. And he was in trouble. He was not a perfect man, not a faultless man. But he was a blameless man in that he never did anything but with a high, pure motive for the glory of God. So, God wants us not to be flawless, but to be blameless. The Lord will overlook flaws within us if He finds consecration to the death and a willingness to serve Him and be His steward, blamelessly, the best that we can. The Lord will overlook flaws. . . .

I ask you to notice one thing here that is in glaring contrast with our usual way of judging things. Do you notice that intellectual qualifications are completely missing? That's strange. Unless where it says, "by sound doctrine both to exhort and to convince." That would assume at least a fair degree of intellectual power. But the qualifications here are not intellectual. They are not what we would call gifted men in the human way of looking at it.

Paul says that they are to be blameless. And then he defines blameless as meaning in our domestic relationships.

A FAITHFUL HUSBAND

The first thing about this man that's mentioned is that he must be the husband of one wife. That is, he was to be monogamous. That means he was to have one wife and not have a cluster of them as they did in many parts of the world then and as they do in many parts of the world now. And Crete being the kind of place it was, being a melding pot for every sort of nationality, philosophy, religion, and race, I can understand how polygamy and the easy getting rid of one wife and taking up of another was common there. It was accepted. Now Paul said, "We are introducing a standard of morals infinitely higher than anything known in Crete." And while he didn't press it, he put it down as a rule. He said that, "If any are to be blameless, the ruler, the bishop, the elder, must be blameless in this that he is a monogamist, not a polygamist. He is the husband of one wife." Somebody asked a Mormon missionary about this, and he said, "Well that means at least one wife." But what it says here is not "at least one wife," but it says, "One wife." That's it. The leader in church affairs, no matter what he does, if he is before the public and the public takes him as an example, he must understand that he owes it to God and to the faith and to the people that he is to be right in this particular.

A FAITHFUL FATHER

Then too, he is to keep a decent house. It says here, "having faithful children not accused of riot or unruly." And I got a smile out of reading Wesley's translation of this. He says, "Having faithful children not accused of luxury or unruly." Wesley was a great believer in a stern, lean way of serving God. He didn't believe in any excess fat, in excess anything. So, instead of the word "riot," he put the word "luxury" in there. "I think that was as close as he thought he could get to the Greek."

So what does it mean here? Some people have been so conscientious about this, that if all their family wasn't converted, they wouldn't serve in the church. They said, "Oh no, I wouldn't serve because all my family is not all converted." Well now, I can't make that mean this. I can only make it to mean that the man who has been given position in the church should not have a reputation of running a loose house, with his children coming in at all hours, drinking and smoking and rioting. The Christian home should be a decent place to live. And if you can't get them all born again, at least you can say to them as I've said a hundred times to mine, "Now remember, the rules of the home are such that if you are staying under the roof, you obey the rules. There are some things that we don't do here. No dancing here, no smoking here, no drinking here, no bad language here. This must be a decent home, a clean place."

I believe that it is this [decency] that Paul has in mind. For instance, if an elder in the church has lost complete control of his family, and his wife pushes him around like a carpet sweeper, and his family won't listen to him, and he is pushed around, and they come in in all hours and the place reeks with smoke and is sacred with drink. Even though the man may be a good man and weep long hours of prayer over this, he ought not, nevertheless, to be in a place of leadership, because people are likely to judge him by his house. And it says here he is not to have a riotous house or an unruly house, but that his children should be faithful and not accused of riot and unruly. What goes on in the hearts of his children he can't help. But he can help what goes on in his home. And a man who doesn't have enough gumption to see that his home is right doesn't have enough of what it takes to be a leader in the church. For it takes not only soft spirituality to be a leader in the church, it takes an ability, as I am going to say tonight, to say, "No" and "Yes."

NOT SELF-WILLED

The third thing about this man is in verse 7: He is not self-willed—that is, he is not a headstrong fellow who will have his way if it busts up the whole church. There is no sense in that—absolutely none. I know a brother who considers himself right in everything, as I do, and I suppose you do. He makes a point of it, and he'll fight it. And even the tiniest little thing. If he said, "I think the chair should be set at this angle," and the deacon said, "No, I think it should be set at that angle," he'd make a church split out of that. He'd divide over that. He is going to tell everyway, everything. Well, that is being self-willed.

We had a word out on the farm. I don't know if they use it in cities or not, but we called a man like that "bull-headed." A bull-headed man has no place in the pulpit. I suppose one of the most bull-headed men that ever lived was Martin Luther, but he had to get over that. He had to come to a place where he said, "Luther died, and the Lord lives within." And though it was normal for him to be strong-willed, he had to humble himself and learn to work with people. My entire ministry has been a self-contradictory affair. It has been this, a temperament that wants to take orders from nobody and get along with nobody, and yet a Scripture conviction that I ought to! So I do. My whole life has consisted, my public ministry has consisted, of walking on a face of a man named Tozer. Our English father was so self-willed and so independent that when he left the farm and came to the city to work for a boss, he resented that boss telling him what to do. He resented him until he died. He didn't want anybody pushing him around.

Well, that is the way I feel by temperament, but the doctrine, the Spirit, and the teaching of the Word tells me that I can't get away with that, that I have to be voted down sometimes, and that my opinions sometime have to get slaughtered. I say on the New York board that if they want something killed, just let me make a speech in favor of it. I and R. Brown, we are two fellas who all we have to do is get up and make a speech and favor something, and they'll vote her flat. Well, I have to learn. The Lord does that to keep me humble. He does that to keep me down. We are not to be self-willed. Nobody. A self-willed superintendent won't get along with his teachers; a self-willed teacher won't get along with his class; a self-willed deacon won't get along with anybody.

NOT EASILY ANGERED

Then in verse 7, another one: not having a bad temper, "not soon angry." We had a preacher come to us incidentally from Salvation Army and become an Alliance preacher. He was an eradication-ist—that is, he believed when you are sanctified, the root of evil went out, and you were perfectly clean, as in before the fall. And he sat on his board one night and some of the deacons brought up something that he didn't agree with, and they got into an argument, and he lost his temper, got red-faced and hot and sassed back. "Oh what am I going to do," he said. "What am I going to do? I taught eradication and a sanctified, clean heart, yet here I am. I got mad and lost my temper and blew up on my own board." I never knew what the brother did. I was always too embarrassed to press it. I never found out. But I do know one thing: you don't have to believe in eradication to get rid of a bad temper. There is no excuse for a bad temper, none in the whole wide world.

Let nobody say, "Yes, but I'm Irish." It doesn't make any difference. God can take the hottest red-headed Irish man that ever lived, calm him and cool him and bless him and fix him. Imagine Tom Hare getting mad and blowing up in your face. You can't think of it, you just can't imagine it, because God has done something for him. But that red-headed fellow was red before it was grey, and I can imagine that before he was saved, if a pipe wrench fell off the pipe, he could yell out an Irish oath like anybody else because he had a temper. If you have a bad temper, consider it a blemish of character. Go to God, deal with it, pray it through, weep it through until God delivers you from it.

Now as dear old brother Dyke used to say when the Lord filled him with the Holy Ghost, he said, "He didn't take the temper out of me, but He took the devil out of my temper." The temper in my saw, my father used to boast about it. He'd say, "That's a fine-tempered saw." He meant it was a finely tempered piece of steel. The quality of it lay in its temper. So, a man with a high temper, he isn't to have that pulled out and promptly be meek and spineless. But he is to have it purified and consecrated, so what used to be a temper that would make him blow up now is an inward strength of character that makes him love righteousness and hate iniquity. He is stronger for that, but when the devil is in it, he's just got an evil temper. And an evil temper always is bad, and there is no excuse for it. And if you've got one, you have no excuse for it under God. Nobody has any right to let himself get elected to anything in any church if he has a bad temper.

NOT ADDICTED TO ALCOHOL

Then he said in verse 7, he is not addicted to alcohol: "not given to wine." "Given to wine" is just a way of saying not given to alcohol. I don't think I need to press that here.

NOT VIOLENT

Well then there is "no striker." This is almost funny, but you have to remember who he is writing to. He is writing to the Cretans. And evidently, the way some people got their way in Crete was to use their fists. That's actually what it means. It has no reference whatsoever to going on strike, like when the International Harvester employees strike. That is another meaning of the word. What it means here is using your fists to strike a blow. Well, it is almost humorous, isn't it, to think of an old deacon trying to get somebody else to do what he is told, and he wouldn't do it, so he just cuffs him to get him to obey? That seems to me like that would be just a little bit extreme. Yet they tell me they want to do that on the foreign field. Some of those heathens just converted, and they get into some little position in the church. And they get their way by using their fists, and they have to learn that that is no way to do it. No way to do it at all. Thank God you don't have to cuff people around to get obedience. The church has found other ways to get obedience. Purgatory is one of them. They say, "I won't pray your grandmother out of hell if you don't be good." But it is about the same thing. I don't know which would be the worst, which morally before God would be the most preposterous. For me to say to McAfee,* "Now, McAfee, go make that call, or I'll black your eye," or to say, "Go make that call, or I'll not pray your mother out of purgatory," it is the same, you know. It is using force, a different kind of force, but it's force. It says, "Don't be any striker."

NOT A LOVER OF MONEY

Then Paul says he ought to not be a lover of money, "not given to filthy lucre." I can hear Paul, when he uses that word, kind

---

*Raymond McAfee was Tozer's longtime associate.

of throwing it off his tongue. He never had any money. Now money is one thing, and filthy money is another. Lucre of course means gain, and filthy lucre means gain that has been gotten filthily or is loved unduly and therefore becomes filthy. You can earn a dollar or ten dollars honestly, and then get a moral attitude toward it that makes it filthy. So money is filthy only when you have made it filthy by your attitude toward it. . . .

The word "gain" in the Scriptures is not a bad word. The Scripture says that a man should seek gain. That is, he should work. If he is a farmer, he should till his soil. The book of Proverbs has many sharp things to say against a man who lies around and lets the grass and weeds grow and doesn't till his soil. Paul has some sharp things to say about the fellow who went from house to house, loafed around, and wouldn't work. He said that everybody ought to work in order that they might have to give to them that are in need, the sick, the poor.

There is nothing here said against honest gain. But when it becomes lucre, then it is filthy. An honest paycheck isn't filthy. An honest increase in your farm income isn't filthy. *Lucre*— incidentally, that is the same word from which *lucrative* comes. We say we want our sons or daughters to have lucrative jobs. Well, the word *lucrative* is not bad, but the word *lucre* is bad. Strange how language goes. But this word *lucre* here almost means "loot," not quite, but almost. It means money that is received beyond the proper amount and particularly money received in an attitude of drooling, covetous delight. That is filthy. It is not the money that is filthy; it is the attitude that makes it so. Now everybody ought to know that a man of God, if he loves money, is not a man of God. Jesus said plainly that we are not to love it, that we are to ask our heavenly Father, and He would take care of us. We were to give freely and not worry about it. The Lord knew, and the Father would take care of us, and He has always done that.

HOSPITABLE

Now verse 8, Paul says that he is to be hospitable. "Hospitable"—what does it mean? Well, it follows, according to all that I can learn, the customs of those days. Custom in those days, missionaries and workers like Paul and Silas and Barnabas and Mark and such traveled from place to place. Paul names many of them in his letters. They went from place to place, and they traveled on a shoestring practically. They were always under pressure, and there was never a red carpet rolled out for them. Somebody grabbed a grey rock instead of a red carpet and was ready to throw rocks. They were always in trouble. And when they got into a town, they couldn't go to a hotel, granted there were any. If there was a hotel in the neighborhood, they couldn't go to it. So the Christians threw their homes open to these traveling preachers.

Here is what hospitality meant: It didn't mean invite your relatives in. That is something to do, and that is good to do. But it is just taken for granted that that's alright for your relatives to visit and exchange visits and have them come and go. Now this "hospitable," according to all the commentators and translators, seems to refer to the way they did it then, traveling about, and they threw their homes open to the traveling preacher. John, you remember, warns against throwing their home open to the wrong kind of preacher. He said if you throw your home open to a false teacher, you've partaken in his evil deeds, you've contributed to his delinquency. So here is hospitality.

A LOVER OF GOOD

Verse 8: he's "a lover of good men." Sometimes the translators don't know whether an adjective "good" or "evil" means an abstraction or a personality. For instance, in the Lord's Prayer, "Deliver us from evil." Translators don't know whether "evil" is a noun or an adjective. They don't know whether that should be "Deliver us from the evil one" or "Deliver us from evil." Either way, it doesn't matter. Here again they are troubled. They don't know whether Paul said, "A lover of good men," or, "a lover of good." But in either case, it's alright because it simply means that man's one qualification as a worker in the church is that he loves good and naturally loves good people.

The question is, "Where is your affinity?" Now, I don't ask you where you spend time, because some of you spend time working where everybody is evil, and you can't help it. But where is your affinity? Where would you go if you were free to go where you would? And where do you feel at home? What kind of people do you seek? Worldlings? If worldlings, it ought to be found out, and not a one should be accepted as a good Christian who finds himself at home among worldlings. . . .

There is a middle, twilight zone of lukewarm people. They are good, decent people, and nothing can be said against them. But they aren't going to embarrass you by talking about the Lord too much, and they are not going to suggest that we pray before we part. And nobody is going to bring up a Bible question. They are just going to have a chit-chat in coffee-clutch style. . . .

I can't see how a church can hope to have the blessing of God on it if it tolerates people in places of leadership who are not lovers of good men, who feel at home among lukewarms or worldlings.

SOBER-MINDED

And going on, "sober"—that means "not flighty." I think it has nothing to do with liquor. We dealt with that above when Paul said he was not to be a lover of wine. It means not reckless, not irresponsible, and not excitable. I've talked this over with some of my friends in days gone by here and there. Pastors know this: Gifted people, good people, and yet irresponsible people you just can't trust with leadership. They think it's freedom, but it's not freedom; it's irresponsibility. "Take my yoke upon you" (Matt. 11:29), and they will not wear a yoke. You can't say they are going to hell. They will go to heaven by the grace of God the way we will all go. But they are unbroken colts.

A colt is loveable and lively, but no good because it has not yet worn a harness or a saddle. And then there are Christians a long way from being colts that will just not wear any harnesses. They'll say they don't believe they should because that's contrary to Paul's doctrine of liberty. But Paul was very careful to teach that while we had all kinds of liberty, we must lay all irresponsibility on ourselves for Christ's sake and the sake of the church. But there are those who are not willing to do that. So they are irresponsible, reckless, excitable, somewhat flighty, and while you like them, you can't trust them. There are thousands of them in the churches.

JUST, HOLY, AND TEMPERATE

Then he says "just," verse 8—that is, honest toward every man. Then, "holy"—that is, your relation to God. And "temperate"— that is, your relation to yourself. There we have again that famous triangle: our relationship to God, ourselves, and our fellow men. Paul calls it "soberly, righteously, and godly" further in his epistle. Here he calls it "just, holy, and temperate." The temperate man is the man who is in right relation to himself. The holy man is one who is in right relation to God. And the just man is one who is in right relation to every man.

But you say, "Well, I haven't always been." Well, start now. Get in right relation with every man. You can't even hope to undo all you've done, but you can start now. I love that beautiful part of Scripture, "Behold, I make all things new." Begin here, begin now.

SOUND IN FAITH

Then "sound doctrine." According to Paul here, verse 9, he's got to hold fast the faithful word. We must remember that Paul was not a technical man. He wouldn't crucify on a technicality. He also was not a careless man. This is the age of creedless religion. We don't believe anything particularly, we just love people, we love everybody and love the Lord. So Jews, Catholics, Christians, and Buddhists all gather together around this simple place of worship and fellowship and all going the same direction. So they say.

But Paul said, "Holding fast the faithful word . . . [of] sound doctrine." Paul was a doctrinarian. Don't forget it. He said love was everything, but he also made doctrine to be the direction love took. And out of doctrine sprang love. So the leader in the church has to be a man who holds fast the faithful world. No loose ideas, no personal interpretations, but the faithful word that he might be able by sound doctrine. I said that there is no intellectual qualification mentioned here, unless it was this one, "that he may be able by sound doctrine both to exhort and to convince the gainsayers" (Titus 1:9).

He had to be able to do two things. He had to be able to expound and expose.

Expound is the positive, and expose is the negative. Expound is to tell what the Scripture says, and expose is to show where teachers are wrong. If you want an example of that, go to Galatians or Colossians or 1 John. There were some pretty sharp exposures. So a good leader of the church has got to be informed. And then he needs to have the ability to expound on his teaching in some degree and to show what is wrong so that the people don't end in the woods. Just as sure as you live, a church that gets careless about its doctrine will end in the same place that a man will who gets careless about watching the signs if he's traveling across the country. He will end up somewhere on a dead-end street in a farmer's backyard. The sound doctrine is the clear, marked highway. And while it isn't everything, it leads to God, and it is so vastly important that it dare not be neglected. Every church should be doctrinally sound. And never should we allow a smiling countenance or a friendly broad religious latitudinarianism, a broad expansiveness of thought that takes in everybody. Never allow that to lead you astray. If you take in everybody, pretty soon we will all be down on the same level. And we will all be without God and without sound faith.

PRAY FOR YOUR LEADERS

When you want to pray for a preacher, don't necessarily pray, "Lord, give him success." Pray that the Lord will help him to be the kind of man that he ought to be.

You want to pray for the church? Pray that the leadership might be this kind of leadership, and that that kind of spirit may be found everywhere, among all God's people, delivered from lust, and from noisy houses where the neighbors don't think well of us, from stubborn bull-headedness that tends to split churches and cause trouble, and alcohol or any other kind of bad habits, the habit of using your fist to get your way. And certainly not to be a lover of money.

The church should be an example to all the neighborhood around about. The church ought never take on the complexion of the neighborhood, never should take on the moral complexion of the age in which it lives. The church is separated from the age in which it lives morally as Jesus Christ was separated from Rome. The church should be a separated people.

And all of us should be this: meek and gentle and quiet and kindly and generous people. So that the world around about us can know what kind of people we are, and the very darkness should make the star of our church shine the brighter. We should have that kind of a church from the newest convert to the oldest, most honored elder. We should have that kind of a church.

6

THE CHARACTER OF THE CHURCH

Then Peter stood up with the Eleven,
raised his voice and addressed the crowd.

<small>Acts 2:14</small>

Here was Peter, standing up, and he lifted up—and that should be the business of the church, to stand up and lift up. Peter became a witness on earth, as the church should be, to things in heaven. The church must be a witness to powers beyond the earthly and the human; and because I know this, it is a source of great grief to me that the church is trying to run on its human powers.

Peter testified to something beyond the human and the earthly. Some power that lay beyond the earthly scene was interested in us and was willing to enter and become known to us. That power turns out to be none other than the Spirit of God Himself.

So Peter, witnessing to things he had experienced, wanted to influence, urge, and exhort those who had not yet experienced to enter in.

Now, a plain word here about the Christian church trying to carry on in its own power: That kind of Christianity makes God sick, for it is trying to run a heavenly institution after an earthly manner.

For myself, if I couldn't have the divine power of God, I would quit the whole business. The church that wants God's power will have something to offer besides social clubs, knitting societies, the Boy Scout troops, and all of the other side issues.

If any church is to be a church of Christ, the living, organic member of that redeemed body of which Christ is the Head, then its teachers and its members must strive earnestly and sacrificially with constant prayer to do a number of things.

FIGHT ENCROACHMENT

First, we must strive to make our beliefs and practices New Testament in their content. We must teach and believe New Testament truths, with nothing dragged in from the outside. It means we must be going constantly back to the grass roots.

The men who pioneered our great North American continent took over a wilderness and conquered it. They went out with their axes, cutting down trees, building houses, and then planting corn, potatoes, other vegetables, and grain. You know, when they planted, they didn't go to bed and sleep until time for the harvest. They fought encroachment from the wilderness from the day they planted their corn and the rest of their crops until they harvested them and had them safely in their log barns.

The wilderness encroaches on the fruitful field, and unless there is constant fighting off of this encroachment, there will be little or no harvest.

I think it is exactly the same with the church, for as one of the old saints said, "Never think for a minute that there will be a time when you will not be tempted. He is tempted the most effectively who thinks that he isn't being tempted at all."

Just when we think we are not being tempted, that is the time of danger, and so it is with the church. We lean back on our own laurels and say, "That may be true of some churches, but it is not true of us. We are increased with goods and have need of nothing!" (see Rev. 3:17).

This is to remind us that we must fight for what we have. Our little field of God's planting must have the necessary weapons and plenty of watchmen out there to drive off the crows and all sorts of creatures, to say nothing of the little insects that destroy the crops. We have to keep after them. We must keep our field healthy, and there is only one way to do that, and that is to keep true to the Word of God. We must constantly go back to the grass roots and get the Word into the church.

SEEK THE POWER

In the second place, we must also earnestly, sacrificially, and prayerfully strive to be empowered with that same power that came upon them.

Peter said, "He hath shed forth this, which ye now see and hear" (Acts 2:33). We must live to gear ourselves into things eternal and to live the life of heaven here upon the earth. We must put loyalty to Christ first at any cost. Anything less than that really isn't a Christian church. I would rather be a member of a group that meets in a little room on a side street than to be part of a great going activity that is not New Testament in its doctrine, in its spirit, in its living, in its holiness, in all of its texture and tenor. We need not expect to be popular in such a church, but certain fruits will follow if we make a church that kind of a church.

FRUITS OF A SPIRIT-FILLED CHURCH

Now, let's note some of the characteristics of a Spirit-filled and Spirit-led congregation.

Joy

First, they will be a joyful people.

The history of the Moravians tells how the Holy Spirit came upon this movement one October morning in 1727. They were having communion. They went out joyful from that place, scarcely knowing whether they were on earth or had died and already gone to heaven. That joyfulness was characteristic of the Moravians for one hundred years. They were not just a happy people in the sense of working up their happiness—their joy came from within.

We do have many professing Christians in our day who are not joyful, but they spend time trying to work it up. Now, brethren, I say that when we give God His place in the church, when we recognize Christ as Lord high and lifted up, when we give the Holy Spirit His place, there will be joy that doesn't have to be worked up. It will be a joy that springs like a fountain. Jesus said that it should be a fountain, an artesian well, that springs up from within. That's one characteristic of a Spirit-filled congregation. They will be a joyful people, and it will be easy to distinguish them from the children of the world.

I wonder what the apostle Paul would say if he came down right now and looked us over in our congregations. What if he walked up and down the aisles of our churches, then went to the theater and looked them over, then on to a hockey game, on to the crowds at the shopping center and into the crowded streets? Then when he came back and looked us over again, I wonder if he would see very much difference. But where the church is a spiritual church, filled with the Spirit, we should always be able to distinguish the children of God from the children of the world.

Useful

Also, let us consider that a congregation that is Spirit-filled will be useful to the race of men.

I am not worried about what the critics say about preachers being parasites and the churches not producing anything, but I do believe that the Christian church ought to be useful to the whole community. We can help the neighborhood where we live, and the neighborhood will be better because we are there as witnessing Christians. We don't need to apologize. Actually, they owe us a great debt, for our kind of transformed people keep the crime rate down, and where we have more God-filled, Spirit-filled churches, we are going to have fewer policemen on the street. Wherever there's more godliness, there's less crime.

A Spirit-filled congregation is useful in the neighborhood—useful to the sons of men, even the ones that are not converted.

Influential

In another sense, we are to be influential among the churches as well.

I would like to see a church become so godly, so Spirit-filled that it would have a spiritual influence on all of the churches in the entire area. Paul told some of his people, "ye were ensamples to all that believe" and "in every place your faith to God-ward is spread abroad" (1 Thess. 1:7–8).

It is entirely right that I should hope this of you. I could hope that we might become so Spirit-filled, walking with God, learning to worship, living so clean and so separated that everybody would know it, and the other churches in our area would be blessed on account of it.

It is common knowledge that when Luther carried out his reformation, the Catholic Church was forced to clean up—the moral pressure from Lutheranism brought about change in the Roman Church. When Wesley came and preached throughout England, the Anglican Church was forced to clean up some of the things that were wrong. Methodism was a spiritual force that compelled others to do something about their own condition.

There is no reason why we could not be a people so filled with the Spirit, so joyfully singing His praises and living so clean in our business and home and school, that the people and other churches would know it and recognize it.

The great thing about this is that when we have a Spirit-filled people who can live well, they can also die well. They began to look at the martyrs in the Roman days and said one to another "Behold, these Christians die well!" Recall that old Balaam wanted to die the death of the righteous, but he wouldn't live the life of the righteous. We Christians ought to be able to die well—we should be able to do that if nothing else.

SOME WON'T LIKE IT

But, of course, there are some folks who just won't ever feel at home in a Spirit-filled congregation. Not all men have faith, and there are some who don't want that kind of a church. I will name some of them now.

"Sunday" Christians

The people who put on religion as a well-pressed Sunday garment won't like that kind of a joyful church.

When we have a revival and the blessing of God comes to us and we do get the help we need from God, those who make religion merely a Sunday garment won't like it very well—in fact, they will be disturbed. From the biblical side, we will insist that they live right on Monday morning, and they don't want to do that. They want to keep their religion disengaged from practical living. Their religion is here and their living is over there. On Sunday they go in and polish their religion, but about 11:00 p.m. in the evening, they put it on the shelf. On Monday they go out and live the way they want to live. I refuse to surrender to that kind of thing and to that kind of people. We are to be a church of the living God and not a gathering of the influential and the big shots. The big shots can come if they get on their knees—a big shot on his knees isn't any taller than anyone else, you know.

Comfortable Christians

The people who refuse to let religion endanger them in any way won't like that kind of church and congregation.

They are those who refuse to let their church or their religion or their faith interfere with their pleasures or their own plans. They know about salvation, and they're willing to serve Jesus. They are on their way to heaven, they will make it through—but they are going to have fun on the way there, and they lay their lives out just as a gardener lays out the garden.

We lay out the plans for our own lives and say, "Now, Lord, it is nice to serve You and we love You, Lord, and let's sing a chorus," but we won't change our plans in any way.

But, let me remind you, the cross of Jesus Christ always changes men's plans. The cross of Christ is revolutionary, and if we are not ready to let it be revolutionary in us nor let it cost us anything or control us in any way, we are not going to like a church that takes the things of God seriously.

People want the benefits of the cross but yet they do not want to bow to the control of the cross. They want to take all the cross can offer but they don't want to be under the lordship of Jesus.

"Fun" Christians

The people who expect religion to be fun won't like that kind of a Spirit-filled congregation.

It is my belief that we have just gone through a long period when Christianity was the "funniest" thing on the continent. We have been told over and over that we could have more fun serving Jesus than we could doing anything else in the whole world. It is clean, too—and we don't have a hangover!

We have been taught in some good evangelical circles, "You serve Jesus and you can have all the fun you want, and you won't have that ugly hangover!"

That was Christianity for the sake of fun, Christianity as an entertaining medium. The whole thing is offensive and foul before God Almighty. My brother, the cross of Christ isn't fun, and it never was fun.

There is such a thing as the joy of the Lord, which is the strength of His people (Neh. 8:10); there is such a thing as having "joy unspeakable and full of glory" (1 Peter 1:8), but the idea that Christianity is another form of entertainment is perfectly ridiculous.

When I sing "Amazing grace, how sweet the sound," I am worshiping God Almighty. If you want to call "entertainment" that which they do before the throne when they cry day and night without ceasing, "Holy, holy, holy, LORD God Almighty" (Rev. 4:8), then I am an entertainer. If it isn't entertainment— and it isn't—then I am a worshiper.

The church must worship, beloved! There is more healing joy in five minutes of worship than there is in five nights of revelry. Nobody ever worshiped God and went out and committed suicide as a hangover. Many a man has killed himself because he had just burned himself out trying to have fun. Many a pretty young woman has thrown herself into having fun, and before she is twenty-five she has to have a retread job done on her countenance—she has simply burned herself out.

Oh, how I love to see the grace of God in a face—don't you? I remember being asked to preach to a group of quiet, plainly dressed people, quite separated from the world in many ways and customs. The women had little black hats sitting on top of their heads and their hair was done up in buns. I had a tie on, you know, and I said to the man who was to introduce me, "You know, I'm a Gentile, and I don't know whether they will take me in or not."

He said, "Oh, preach to their hearts, and they will just forget that you don't belong to them." I did just that—and they did just that! I was just absolutely refreshed and wonderfully blessed.

Cultural Christians

Nor will the people who embrace a church for its cultural values be happy and satisfied in a Spirit-filled congregation.

Have you ever met these people? They don't know anything about the Spirit in their lives or the Spirit-filled church. They do believe the cultural value of the church is good for them and offers them something, and they want their children brought up in the cultural atmosphere of the church. They want book reviews and lectures on flower arrangements and child-rearing and all sorts of things—but it is a foregone conclusion that they are not going to be at home among God's dear regenerated people who are intent upon spiritual advance.

So, we will always have to be aware that this kind of discontent is going to rule out a few, and we are made sad by their decision. But we thank God for those who will be in their glory if we go constantly to the grass roots, weeding out everything that is not of God and keeping the grain growing lush and beautiful. Thank God for those who want to gear into things heavenly and walk with God and obey the truth and love each other!

WHO WILL THRIVE IN A SPIRIT-FILLED CHURCH?

Who are these people who will be happy and contented and fulfilled in a Spirit-filled congregation?

They Want to Be Rid of Their Sins

They are those who want to be rid of their sins. If I had a cancer growing on my neck I would want to be rid of it—the sooner the better. No one could come to me and say, "Now, I have a cowbell—let me shake it. Don't you like it?"

I would say, "No, I don't like it—I'm interested in this cancer on my neck. Do you have a cure for it?"

You say, "Aw, let's forget the cancer—let me jingle the bell."

Sometimes we have this kind in the church, but they are of no help. Let's talk about getting rid of our sins. Some people that are overwhelmed with the desire to be free from their sins have had refining fire go through their hearts sanctifying the whole. These people will be happy among us.

They Desire to Know God

The people who want to know God and to walk with God will be happy here, too. Their ambition is to walk with God and to "follow the Lamb whithersoever he goeth" (Rev. 14:4). The Lord's people know and appreciate one another. We may get an occasional bad apple—Jesus had Judas Iscariot in His little flock. We know each other and when we shake hands and someone says something to us about God, we sort of know we are talking to a brother in Christ. No matter what our backgrounds or where we came from—we all talk the same language if we are brothers and sisters in Jesus Christ, our Lord. We know and appreciate one another.

They Hear His Voice

Then, too, those who have learned to recognize the voice of the good Shepherd will be at home in a Spirit-filled church.

It is sad, to us, that some people have never heard the voice of the Shepherd. His voice is as tender as a lullaby and as strong as the wind and as mighty as "the sound of many waters" (1:15). The people who have learned to hear and recognize the voice of Jesus—that healing, musical, solemn, beautiful voice of Jesus in His church—are always at home where everything centers around Him.

The true Christian church can be a conglomeration of everything under the sun. That is, we may have Calvinists and Arminians and Methodists and Baptists and all sorts of people, and yet we are all together on one thing—Jesus Christ is wisdom, righteousness, sanctification, and redemption! He is All in all, and the people of the Lord who have learned to hear the voice of the Shepherd gravitate toward that kind of church.

They Sense His Presence

Then, there are those who are sensitive to the Invisible

Presence, and they will be at home in this group.

They may not be so sure about who else is present, but they know the Lord is present, and they are sensitive to that.

Do you find your own heart sensitive to the Lord's presence, or are you among those who are "samplers" and "nibblers"? God help you if you are, for the child of the King isn't a sampler and a nibbler—he's a sheep who loves his Shepherd, and he stays close to his Shepherd. That's the only safe place for a sheep—at the Shepherd's side, because the devil doesn't fear sheep—he just fears the Shepherd. Your spiritual safety and well-being lies in being near to the Shepherd. Stay close to Jesus and all the wolves in the world cannot get a tooth in you.

There are those who have tasted of the good Word of God and felt the mysterious power of the world to come. Thank God for those in the churches who would rather hear the voice of Jesus than the voice of the greatest preacher or the best singer in the world. Thank God for those who would rather be conscious of the divine presence than be in the presence of the greatest man in the world. Thank God for those who are sick of their own sin and long to be holy—I pray that your numbers may increase.

These are the things in which we believe: Jesus Christ the Lord; clean living, decency and separation from all things that are wrong; joyful, radiant, happy worship; sweet fellowship based on kindliness and patience, endurance and honesty. We believe in the missionary outlook, and above all things, "worship the LORD in the beauty of holiness" (1 Chron. 16:29).

7

THE UNITY
OF THE CHURCH

So in Christ we, though many, form one body,
and each member belongs to all the others.

ROMANS 12:5

Nothing in the whole world is quite so wonderfully made as the human body, and it is no small wonder that the Holy Spirit said through David, "I am fearfully and wonderfully made" (Ps. 139:14). The hands, the ears, the sense of smell, the sense of taste, the sense of touch, feet and hands all working together—only the creative wisdom and power of God can account for the amazing human body.

I call your attention to the fact that in three of his epistles, the apostle Paul used the members of the physical body to illustrate the spiritual relationships in the body of Christ, the church. He used the body-member relationship in Romans, in 1 Corinthians, and in Ephesians.

In Romans 12, Paul, being a great illustrator, broke things down for us so that we could easily understand when he said that the church is a body—Christ is the head and the true Christian is a member of that body.

Now, the Holy Spirit is to the church what your spirit is to the body that God has given you. It is the life, the union, the consciousness—and as each member recapitulates the local church, each local church recapitulates the entire church of Christ, Paul asserts.

ALL ONE BODY

What Paul is emphasizing is the fact that the church, the body of Christ, is not torn nor divided, but each local church group has all the functions of the whole body. Just as each individual state is a vital, throbbing part of the whole union of the states, so each local church is a living, organic part of the whole church of Christ. I believe that we are members of the whole body of Christ in heaven and all over the world, but we all are descendants of the great God, who by the Holy Spirit and the Word caused us to be born into His family.

Therefore, the church of Christ is not divided.

When we sing that old song, "We are not divided, all one body we," people smile and say, "How about your six hundred denominations?"

Well, they don't frustrate me with that question. That song, that truth—"We are not divided, all one body we"—is just as true as the fact that I am not divided. The body of Christ is all one body. We can sing it, and let those people make fun of us if they will—keep on singing it, for it is true!

We are not divided. It is a whole church. Everyone who has ever been born into the family of God is born into a living, organic union, and there we are. There is nothing the devil can do about it.

Each local group, I say, has all the functions of the whole group, just as the body of each man has all of the human faculties and organs and members. The members are designed so that each has a function. The eyes are designed to see, the ears to hear, the hands to do work, the feet for movement, the stomach to digest food, and so on.

So, we are designed to cooperate, and that's in concert. I remember once reading a great article in *Harper's* magazine. It explained what brought on old age. It said it was not the loss of strength in any organ of the body, but that the organs of the body ceased to cooperate and went off on their own, and that was what brought on old age. It was the failure of the organs of the body to cooperate that made people die of old age. They got independent and went off and started their own tabernacle, if we can use it in that sense of illustration!

So it is with the church. When we work together and have a sense of unity and fellowship, when we all work together, cooperate with each other, and act in concert, when all are for each and each for all, and all take directions from the Head, then one has a perfect church. Each local church can sum it up, and we can all sum it up ourselves.

NOT ALL DIVISIONS ARE BAD

When to unite and when to divide, that is the question, and a right answer requires the wisdom of a Solomon.

Some settle the problem by rule of thumb: All union is good and all division bad. It's that easy. But obviously this effortless way of dealing with the matter ignores the lessons of history and overlooks some of the deep spiritual laws by which men live.

If good men were all for union and bad men for division, or vice versa, that would simplify things for us. Or if it could be shown that God always unites and the devil always divides it would be easy to find our way around in this confused and confusing world. But that is not how things are.

To divide what should be divided and unite what should be united is the part of wisdom. Union of dissimilar elements is never good even where it is possible, nor is the arbitrary division of elements that are alike; and this is as certainly true of things moral and religious as of things political or scientific.

The first divider was God who at the creation divided the light from the darkness. This division set the direction for all God's dealings in nature and in grace. Light and darkness are incompatible; to try to have both in the same place at once is to try the impossible and end by having neither the one nor the other, but dimness, rather, and obscurity.

In the world of men there are at present scarcely any sharp outlines. The race is fallen. Sin has brought confusion. The wheat grows with the tares, the sheep and the goats coexist, the farms of the just and the unjust lie side by side in the landscape, the mission is next door to the saloon.

But things will not always be so. The hour is coming when the sheep will be divided from the goats and the tares separated from the wheat. God will again divide the light from the darkness and all things will run to their kind. Tares will go into the fire with tares and wheat into the garner with wheat. The dimness will lift like a fog and all outlines will appear. Hell will be seen to be hell all the way through, and heaven revealed as the one home of all who bear the nature of the one God.

For that time we with patience wait. In the meanwhile for each of us, and for the church wherever she appears in human society, the constantly recurring question must be: What shall we unite with and from what shall we separate? The question of coexistence does not enter here, but the question of union and fellowship does. The wheat grows in the same field with the tares, but shall the two cross-pollinate? The sheep graze near the goats, but shall they seek to interbreed? The unjust and the just enjoy the same rain and sunshine, but shall they forget their deep moral differences and intermarry?

To these questions the popular answer is yes. Union for union's sake, and men shall brothers be for a' that. Unity is so devoutly to be desired that no price is too high to pay for it and nothing is important enough to keep us apart. Truth is slain to provide a feast to celebrate the marriage of heaven and hell, and all to support a concept of unity that has no basis in the Word of God.

The Spirit-illuminated church will have none of this. In a fallen world like ours, unity is no treasure to be purchased at the price of compromise. Loyalty to God, faithfulness to truth, and the preservation of a good conscience are jewels more precious than gold of Ophir or diamonds from the mine. For these jewels men have suffered the loss of property, imprisonment, and even death; for them, even in recent times, behind the various curtains, followers of Christ have paid the last full measure of devotion and quietly died, unknown to and unsung by the great world, but known to God and dear to His Father heart. In the day that shall declare the secrets of all souls these shall come forth to receive the deeds done in the body. Surely such as these are wiser philosophers than the religious camp followers of meaningless unity who have not the courage to stand against current vogues and who bleat for brotherhood only because it happens to be for the time popular.

"Divide and conquer" is the cynical slogan of Machiavellian political leaders, but Satan knows also how to *unite* and conquer. To bring a nation to its knees, the aspiring dictator must unite it. By repeated appeals to national pride or to the need to avenge some past or present wrong, the demagogue succeeds in uniting the populace behind him. It is easy after that to take control of the military and to beat the legislature into submission. Then follows almost perfect unity indeed, but it is the unity of the stockyards and the concentration camp. We have seen this happen several times in this century, and the world will see it at least once more when the nations of the earth are united under Antichrist.

When confused sheep start over a cliff the individual sheep can save himself only by separating from the flock. Perfect unity at such a time can only mean total destruction for all. The wise sheep to save his own hide disaffiliates.

Power lies in the union of things similar and the division of things dissimilar. Maybe what we need in religious circles today is not more union but some wise and courageous division. Everyone desires peace, but it could be that revival will follow the sword.

THE COMMUNION OF THE CHURCH

I believe in . . . the communion of saints.

<small>Apostles' Creed</small>

It would be difficult if not altogether impossible for us [today] to know exactly what was in the minds of the church fathers who introduced [these] words into the creed, but in the Book of Acts we have a description of the first Christian communion: "Then they that gladly received his word were baptized: and the same day there were added unto them about three thousand souls. And they continued steadfastly in the apostles' doctrine and fellowship, and in breaking of bread, and in prayers" (2:41–42).

Here is the original apostolic fellowship, the pattern after which every true Christian communion must be modeled.

The word "fellowship," in spite of its abuses, is still a beautiful and meaningful word. When rightly understood it means the same as the word "communion"—that is, the act and condition of sharing together in some common blessing by numbers of persons. The communion of saints, then, means an intimate and loving sharing together of certain spiritual blessings by persons who are on an equal footing before the blessing in which they share. This fellowship must include every member of the church of God from Pentecost to this present moment and on to the end of the age.

Now, before there can be *communion* there must be *union*. The sharers are one in a sense altogether above organization, nationality, race, or denomination. That oneness is a divine thing, achieved by the Holy Spirit in the act of regeneration. Whoever is born of God is one with everyone else who is born of God. Just as gold is always gold, wherever and in whatever shape it is found, and every detached scrap of gold belongs to the true family and is composed of the same elements, so every regenerate soul belongs to the universal Christian community and to the fellowship of the saints.

Every redeemed soul is born out of the same spiritual life as every other redeemed soul and partakes of the divine nature in exactly the same manner. Each one is thus made a member of the Christian community and a sharer in everything which that community enjoys. This is the true communion of saints. But to know this is not enough. If we would enter into the power of it we must exercise ourselves in this truth; we must *practice* thinking and praying with the thought that we are members of the body of Christ and brothers to all the ransomed saints living and dead who have believed on Christ and acknowledged Him as Lord.

We have said that the communion of saints is a fellowship, a sharing in certain divinely given things by divinely called persons. Now, what are those things?

FELLOWSHIP OF LIFE

The first and most important is *life*—"the life of God in the soul of man," to borrow a phrase from Henry Scougal. This life is the basis of everything else that is given and shared. And that life is nothing else than God Himself. It should be evident that there can be no true Christian sharing unless there is first an impartation of life. An organization and a name do not make a church. One hundred religious persons knit into a unity by careful organization do not constitute a church any more than eleven dead men make a football team. The first requisite is life, always.

FELLOWSHIP OF TRUTH

The apostolic fellowship is also a fellowship of *truth*. The inclusiveness of the fellowship must always be held along with the exclusiveness of it. Truth brings into its gracious circle all who admit and accept the Bible as the source of all truth and the Son of God as the Savior of men. But there dare be no weak compromise with the facts, no sentimental mouthing of the old phrases: "We are all headed for the same place. Each one is seeking in his own way to please the Father and make heaven his home." The truth makes men free, and the truth will bind and loose, will open and shut, will include and exclude at its high will without respect to persons. To reject or deny the truth of the Word is to exclude ourselves from the apostolic communion.

Now, someone may ask, "What is the truth of which you speak? Is my fate to depend upon Baptist truth or Presbyterian truth or Anglican truth, or all of these or none of these? To know the communion of saints must I believe in Calvinism or Arminianism? In the Congregational or the Episcopal form of church government? Must I interpret prophecy in accord with the premillenarians or the postmillenarians? Must I believe in immersion or sprinkling or pouring?" The answer to all this is easy. The confusion is only apparent, not actual.

The early Christians, under the fire of persecution, driven from place to place, sometimes deprived of the opportunity for careful instruction in the faith, wanted a "rule" that would sum up all that they must believe to assure their everlasting welfare. Out of this critical need arose the creeds. Of the many, the Apostles' Creed is the best known and best loved, and has been reverently repeated by the largest number of believers through the centuries. And for millions of good men, that creed contains the essentials of truth. Not all truths, to be sure, but the heart of all truth. It served in trying days as a kind of secret password that instantly united men to each other when passed from lip to lip by the followers of the Lamb. It is fair to say, then, that the truth shared by saints in the apostolic fellowship is the same truth that is outlined for convenience in the Apostles' Creed.

In this day, when the truth of Christianity is under serious fire from so many directions, it is most important that we know what we believe and that we guard it carefully. But in our effort to interpret and expound the Holy Scriptures in accord with the ancient faith of all Christians, we should remember that a seeking soul may find salvation through the blood of Christ while yet knowing little of the fuller teachings of Christian theology. We must, therefore, admit to our fellowship every sheep who has heard the voice of the Shepherd and has tried to follow Him.

The beginner in Christ who has not yet had time to learn much Christian truth, and the underprivileged believer who has had the misfortune to be brought up in a church where the Word has been neglected from the pulpit, are very much in the same situation. Their faith grasps only a small portion of truth, and their "sharing" is necessarily limited to the small portion they grasp. The important thing, however, is that the little bit they do enjoy is *real truth*. It may be no more than this, that "Christ Jesus came into the world to save sinners" (1 Tim. 1:15); but if they walk in the light of that much truth, no more is required to bring them into the circle of the blessed and to constitute them true members of the apostolic fellowship.

FELLOWSHIP OF PRESENCE

Then, true Christian communion consists in the sharing of a *presence*. This is not poetry merely, but a fact taught in bold letters in the New Testament. God has given us Himself in the person of His Son. "Where two or three are gathered together in my name, there am I in the midst of them" (Matt. 18:20). The immanence of God in His universe makes possible the enjoyment of the "real presence" by the saints of God in heaven and on earth simultaneously. Wherever they may be, He is present to them in the fullness of His Godhead.

I do not believe that the Bible teaches the possibility of communication between the saints on earth and those in heaven.

But while there cannot be communication, there most surely can be communion. Death does not tear the individual believer from his place in the body of Christ. As in our human bodies each member is nourished by the same blood that at once gives life and unity to the entire organism, so in the body of Christ the quickening Spirit flowing through every part gives life and unity to the whole. Our Christian brethren who have gone from our sight retain still their place in the universal fellowship. The church is one, whether waking or sleeping, by a unity of life forevermore.

MUTUAL BELONGING

The most important thing about the doctrine of the communion of saints is its practical effects on the lives of Christians. We know very little about the saints above, but about the saints on earth we know, or can know, a great deal. We Protestants do not believe (since the Bible does not teach) that the saints who have gone into heaven before us are in any way affected by the prayers or labors of saints who remain on earth. Our particular care is not for those whom God has already honored with the vision beatific, but for the hard-pressed and struggling pilgrims who are still traveling toward the City of God. We all belong to each other; the spiritual welfare of each one is or should be the loving concern of all the rest.

We should pray for an enlargement of soul to receive into our hearts all of God's people, whatever their race, color, or church affiliation. Then we should practice thinking of ourselves as members of the blessed family of God and should strive in prayer to love and appreciate everyone who is born of the Father.

I suggest also that we try to acquaint ourselves as far as possible with the good and saintly souls who lived before our times and now belong to the company of the redeemed in heaven. How sad to limit our sympathies to those of our own day, when God in His providence has made it possible for us to enjoy the rich treasures of the minds and hearts of so many holy and gifted saints of other days. To confine our reading to the works of a few favorite authors of today or last week is to restrict our horizons and to pinch our souls dangerously.

I have no doubt that the prayerful reading of some of the great spiritual classics of the centuries would destroy in us forever that constriction of soul that seems to be the earmark of modern evangelicalism.

For many of us the wells of the past wait to be reopened. Augustine, for instance, would bring to us a sense of the overwhelming majesty of God that would go far to cure the flippancy of spirit found so widely among modern Christians. Bernard of Cluny would sing to us of "Jerusalem the Golden" and the peace of an eternal sabbath day until the miserable pleasures of this world become intolerable; Richard Rolle would show us how to escape from "the abundance of riches, the flattering of women and the fairness of youth," that we may go on to know God with an intimacy that will become in our hearts "heat, fragrance and song"; Tersteegen would whisper to us of the "hidden love of God" and the awful presence until our hearts would become "still before Him" and "prostrate inwardly adore Him"; before our eyes the sweet St. Francis would throw his arms of love around sun and moon, trees and rain, bird and beast, and thank

God for them all in a pure rapture of spiritual devotion.

But who is able to complete the roster of the saints? To them we owe a debt of gratitude too great to comprehend: prophet and apostle, martyr and reformer, scholar and translator, hymnist and composer, teacher and evangelist, not to mention ten thousand times ten thousand simplehearted and anonymous souls who kept the flame of pure religion alive even in those times when the faith of our fathers was burning but dimly all over the world.

They belong to us, all of them, and we belong to them. They and we and all redeemed men and women of whatever age or clime are included in the universal fellowship of Christ, and together compose "a royal priesthood, an holy nation, a peculiar people" (1 Peter 2:9), who enjoy a common but blessed communion of saints.

THE FREEDOM OF THE CHURCH

So if the Son sets you free, you will be free indeed.

JOHN 8:36

The lack of freedom in the church of Christ is one of the greatest hindrances of the church. Now, I'll tell you why.

There is a dark and sinister foe whose name is the devil and Satan, that old dragon, who is busy, dedicated to our damnation. Or if we are Christians, I think even the devil knows there is no use to try to damn a Christian. Now I don't know whether the devil is a Calvinist, but I do know that the devil knows that when a child of God is in the hands of God and justification is his, I think even the devil knows he can't damn him. But he does want to keep his spirit imprisoned. That is the business of the devil. It is to either keep our spirit imprisoned or change our figure. If he can't prevent us from being alive, then he keeps us wound up with grave clothes that we might almost as well be dead. And thus, he robs us of our heritage.

We are like sons of a fabulously wealthy man who has died and willed all of his millions to us. And still, we go around in rags and, with an old stick, poke through cast-off crust and sing to our Father in heaven while we munch on the crust with our gums and while a chill wind bites through our ragged clothing and our toes show through our battered shoes.

But we are rich, nevertheless, rich as Midas, richer than King Solomon in Christ Jesus. But we are not doing anything about it because Satan is busy, dedicated either to keeping us lost—and he hasn't succeeded in that if you are a Christian—or to keeping you bound.

DEFIED BY THE DEVIL

Now, I don't believe a Christian can be possessed by evil spirits. But he can be spirit-oppressed and intimidated and silenced and repressed. And this is the work of the devil, to repress and silence.

A man told me he was preaching in a series of meetings in a certain church, and there were two spiritists. And these peepers and mutterers—two women—they decided to silence him. They didn't like the way he was talking, and they were coming to that church, and they decided they were going to silence him. So they figured it out, and one of them sat to his left and the other sat to his right, and they got him touched with the spirits. And he said he had never struggled so in his preaching. He said he didn't know what it was. He couldn't understand it, but a shadow came over his heart and a sense of confusion. And he had no urge and no eloquence and no lift. And he was beaten down and oppressed, and he said he couldn't understand it. And one evening as he was preaching, he suddenly said, "Jesus' victor! Thou art at the right hand of the Father." He said that something instantly snapped, and he was a free man. Those two women cleared out and never came back. They couldn't take Jesus.

Now if you think that is fanaticism, think on. I don't. I believe that to be perfectly, legitimately, entirely scriptural. The devil wants to keep us frightened and silenced and intimidated, so that if we are alive, we are just barely alive.

If you remember, back in the Valley of Elah, the valley that lay between Israel and the Philistines, Saul—sour, old Saul, fearful, intimidated Saul—was leading Israel. But everybody was scared because a great giant was going about beating his chest and saying, "I defy the armies of Israel this day" (1 Sam. 17:10).

And a little fellow by the name of David came along, and David told Israel, "Let no man's heart fail because of him; thy servant will go and fight with this Philistine" (1 Sam. 17:32).

That was the first encouragement Israel had. There they were. They were alive. They were God's people. They were God's soldiers. But they were intimidated so that they couldn't open their mouths, and they gazed in fascinated fear at that great giant as he defied them. And I believe that any church that wants to make any progress has got to face this. It is defied immediately by the devil.

I find some Christians who are just childishly happy about everything. They are just children playing in the marketplaces. But once you get serious about this and you determine that you are going to have all God has for you on this earth—die or live, or sink or swim—you are up against raw hell immediately. And the devil is not going to let you off easy.

Now, we are a flock of frightened sheep. There is no question about it. You are so scared that you can't even say, "Amen," only one or two in the whole congregation. You say, "Well, you don't give me time." Maybe that is partly it, but some of you could be given until Judgment Day, and you wouldn't get an "Amen" squeezed out because you would be afraid of what people would think of you. We are a flock of frightened sheep.

Jesus Christ came down, took our body on Himself. And now if Jesus was here, He might be a little taller, a little heavier, or a little differently built, but He would be generally like I am and like you are. He was a man, a very man, born of a woman, a man wearing our nature, but He was also God, and He went out on a cross, and there they crucified Him. God Almighty sacrificed Him as the one last, final fulfillment of all the sacrifices that had ever been made on Jewish altars. And after He had been three days in the grave, He came out. And after a few days, He ascended to the right hand of God and sat down amidst the acclamations of the heavenly host. And there He sits at God's right hand, a *living* man, our representative there. And we ought to be the most fearless, most relaxed, most utterly self-assured—or God-assured—people of the wide world and the happiest people.

But we are not, nevertheless, because this devil has intimidated us. Like old Goliath, "I defy the armies of Israel." And I hear a sinister, sour voice tonight saying cynically, "I defy you Christians. What can you do? You know you can't do anything!" He may get fooled yet.

We are a flock of frightened sheep, and I don't think we ought to be any longer.

CAPTURED BY FEAR

What are we afraid of?

Well, we are afraid of our past sins. Sin is such a terrible thing, and God knows it is, and we know it is, and the devil knows it is. And he knows how to follow us around, reminding us, "You want to be a happy man? Why look, your sin."

Well, I talk back a little bit, even though I don't recommend this. But I say, "Yes, Devil. Sure. But look, I got it from you!" Everything that is against me, I got from the devil. And everything that is even possible, I got from Jesus Christ.

So why should he have the infinite upfrontry and crass and brass to argue with me about it? He'll do it because he is the devil. If he can't keep us damned, then he keeps us shut in a little cage and keeps our wings clipped so that we never can fly. We claim we believe the sins are gone, but we don't half believe it. We've sung for so many years, "Arise, my soul. Arise. Shake off my guilty fears." But we still go around like the cat I got down at the house. We got a cat. One ran away, so somebody gave us another. And she has been frightened ever since she has been there. Now, she's a nice cat, and we like her, and she is thawing out a little. But she walks around real close to the ground and timid and slinky. And if you just make so much of a noise, she jumps. She is frightened. She's strange.

Well we are just like that in the kingdom of God. We move about strange and cautious and scared. We are afraid of our past sin.

Now, my brethren, why do we say that our sins are gone and then act as if they aren't gone? If they are not gone, why do we say they are? And if they are gone, why do we act as if they are not? You have been declared not guilty by the highest court in all the wide universe. Therefore, why should you go around frightened?

And yet some of you are honest Christians—you deeply seek the face of God and you wouldn't do a wrong in the wide world and you want God more than you want to live—but you still can't get loose. The grave clothes trip you every time you try to run a little faster. Satan uses your past sins to terrify you.

An old man once said, "God forgives a man, then forgets about his sin and refuses to think of it." And he said, "When God forgives a man, He trusts him just the same as if he never sinned." I never heard anyone say that God trusted people. But this man was a master of the inner life, and he said, "When God forgives a man, He doesn't say, 'Well now you ought to watch this fellow because he has a bad record.' He starts as if he had just been created, and as if there had been no past at all."

Now if you can believe that, you might even smile a little bit. But here we are, and old Goliath says, "I defy the armies of that church." Well, he'll say that once too often, but we'll get through to heaven, and God Almighty will help us here yet.

Another thing that intimidates us is memories of our failures. And Satan will never let you forget. You fail, and Satan will come and say, "Now you made a big to-do about the deeper life. And you made a big to-do about wanting to be filled with the Spirit and live the life in the Spirit. And yet look at the flops you made. Look how many times you bruised yourself tumbling around."

The Bible says that if a man falls seven times, he rises. The matter isn't that you fell, it is whether you allow the devil to charge you with that.

Look at the man they called a seraphic Fletcher.* Seven times he fell and failed God. Seven times. Then he came out of the room, saying, "Now, God, I believe I am delivered from all sin and if You will help me, I'll never let the world hear the last of it." And that was the end. That was the last time he tumbled.

Now, if our failures are going to hinder us, we might just as well never start in the first place. Did you not know that Jesus Christ, that God when He saved you, knew what kind of a fella you were? Listen to this: "Yea, thou heardest not; yea, thou knewest not; yea, from that time that thine ear was not opened: for I knew that thou wouldest deal very treacherously, and wast called a transgressor from the womb" (Isa. 48:8).

The devil says, "But God doesn't know you like I do. He hasn't watched you as I have. Remember that time, remember that time." That is the devil talking. And God says, "I knew that thou wouldest deal very treacherously, and wast called a transgressor from the womb. For my name's sake will I defer mine anger, and for my praise will I refrain for thee, that I cut thee not off. Behold, I have refined thee, but not with silver; I have chosen thee in the furnace of affliction. For mine own sake, even for mine own sake, will I do *it*" (vv. 9–11).

God has a stake in you. And for His own sake will He do it. Don't you think He didn't know you were treacherous? He knows that the blood of Adam runs through your veins, and it is tainted blood. He knows your nervous system is a hedonic nervous system, aggravated by thousands of years of hereditary

---

*John Fletcher, a Methodist Wesleyan theologian and preacher from Switzerland in the 1700s.

taint. He says, "I knew you were treacherous. I knew you had a heart for it. I knew. But for My own sake, I am doing this thing."

Look away from yourself. God is not going to bless you for your sake. He is going to bless you for Jesus' sake and for the sake of His own name, for His own glorious namesake. If you think that there is anybody in this world good enough that God could do anything for their sake, you don't know sin. And if you think there isn't anything that God won't do for you for His sake, you don't know God.

Don't let your past failures get you down, though there were many and have been many, and aggravating they have been. You have made a fool out of yourself, and your testimony has been punctured, flattened, and spoiled. But don't you ever let that stop you for a second. God knew all about you, and you are not responsible to men. You stand responsibly before your heavenly Father and Jesus Christ at the right hand of God. So don't you let your failures get you down. In our weaknesses, we are all scared stiff because of our weaknesses. We know how weak we are.

And then some of us are frightened sheep because while we stand on the edge of the river, we won't cross. We are at Kadesh Barnea or we are at the River Jordan and are afraid to go across for fear to lose our reputation as a sober Christian.

My old mother-in-law, God bless her memory, had her faults, but she was a great winner of souls. She helped bump many a young fella into the ministry and missionary work. And she used to say, "Be willing to be a fool for Jesus' sake." And she practiced it.

Be willing to be a fool for Jesus' sake. It sounded awful to a young fella who didn't want to be a fool. I wanted to be quite a fine young preacher. But be willing to be a fool for Jesus' sake. I don't know where she got it, but it was good. Most people aren't willing to be fools for Jesus' sake.

Communists will make doubled-eyed long ear junkies out of themselves for the cause that they fight for. Jehovah's Witnesses will be willing to be put into jail, cussed down, put out, and lampooned for the sake of a miserable, twisted doctrine. And we Christians, we are so respectable and smooth. So many of you respectable Christians will never get where you ought to be until God takes away your respectability. We have a name for being "very sound Christians." Our brother knows the Scriptures, and he is very sound. Very sound? I haven't heard a sound anywhere!

We sing Charles Wesley's hymns, but we forget that Charles Wesley was considered a donkey by a lot of the "sound" Christians of his time. We quote Charles G. Finney, but Charles G. Finney was in trouble all of the time with the people who stood around and tried to frown him down. And so with every saint that has ever lived in the world. There is a period when we have to lose our reputation as being a "sound" Christian.

I have often mentioned a man whose Bible conference I attended last summer, and he called me out as soon as he saw me. He said, "Brother, I just want to tell you something." He said, "I used to be one of the most self-assured, cocky young fellows you every saw in your life." I am paraphrasing what he said, but this is the gist of it. He said, "I was doing things the way the church was doing them. I went to Wales." He got talking to some old Welsh people, and they had remembered Evan Roberts. And they told this snappy, self-assured young American Bible conference director and founder about Evan Roberts. It was like unloading a ton of bricks on him. Down he went. He crawled off into a little cottage where he was staying and got down on his knees and sweat it out before God.

And he said, "Mr. Tozer, I don't know what happened, but I was filled with the Holy Ghost, and my whole life is transformed."

He said, "All I want now is that once more in this generation, a cheated, betrayed church should see the glory of God."

He said, "That is all I want. That the church should once more see the glory of God. That is all."

He said, "Now I don't care what happens."

And I said, "Do you realize, brother, that if you carry through on this that you may lose some of your very best fundamentalist friends?"

He said, "I am perfectly willing to lose."

I said, "Do you realize that you'll get a reputation for having gone off your rocker?"

He said, "I don't care. I am perfectly willing."

Now he said, "We brought you here to gives us the best and the worst you got. Give it to us and don't pull any punches."

And I did.

We had a week there. I learned later that five young people met God that week and now are in Bible school. And I am in touch with this brother by letter, and he always writes, "I want you to come, brother. I believe God wants to do something for us." Yet he hasn't changed his doctrine at all! He is just a good ole' Calvinist. He could pass anywhere among the fundamentalists doctrinally. But he wants fire on his doctrine, and he got it. And he completely kicked the foundation out from under his Bible conferences. And he said, "I don't care. If God doesn't run these Bible conferences, I am perfectly willing to lose the whole thing. From now on, no more big financial drives. I am going to ask God to send the money in, and if He doesn't do it, I'll lose the whole business."

If you go on with God, you will lose your reputation for a while, but then it will slowly come back to you. I lost mine some years back, and people even reported that I was a liberal. I don't know how in the world they got that. But they reported, "Tozer's gone liberal" because I stopped talking this stilted, wooded language of the frightened fundamentalist and began to preach up there a little. They said, "He's liberal."

Then there are some who are afraid of fanaticism. Satan goads peoples into violent extremes and fills Christians with a fear of being extreme. Isn't that a funny thing? The devil will give us Elvis Presley and goad people into the violent extremes. I told you that I passed by a hall. Now, I passed by; I was on my way to preach. But I passed by a hall where Presley was. The place was packed and the police were having trouble with the crowds. And in the frightful, erotic fury of that concert, women tore their clothes off. And the police had to grab them and herd them off to the side.

And when the Christian looks up and says, "Amen," the same devil says, "You fanatic! Shut up. You ought to be quiet and sound. Don't you know? You ought to be ashamed of yourself!" Oh what a devil the devil is! And we are a frightened bunch of sheep, scared stiff and jumpy and skittish and filled with caution while we got someone at the right hand of God, and we ought to start acting like it now. . . .

The devil is a liar and the father of lies. He is a murderer, and he never tells the truth unless he can embarrass you with it. The only truth he ever tells is to remind you of how you sinned and how you have fallen and the failures you had. That is truth, but that is truth used to destroy you.

VICTORY IN AN OVERCOMING SAVIOR

There is a nameless inward chill that I can't quite identify, but it is on the church of Christ. We talk about how happy we are: "The shouts of glory roll, the waves of glory roll, the shouts I can't control." We manage to control them pretty well. Some of you come back from a ball game hoarse, but nobody ever goes home from church hoarse. A nameless inward chill that lies like a shadow over our hearts.

Many of you have met and are meeting God's terms. But you are still under the shadow, and you are wearing the grave clothes. But our Moses has come to deliver us, who has gone into heaven and is on the right hand of God, with angels, and authorities, and powers being made subject to Him. We are not dealing with a babe in a manger, and we are not dealing with a man on a cross. Formal Christianity deals with a babe in a manger. Catholicism mainly deals with a man on a crucifix. But the Bible tells us there is a Man on the throne, sitting at the right hand of power, and we are dealing with Him. The babe in the manger was weak; the man on the cross was dead. But the Man on the throne is alive forevermore. And He carries our names on His shoulders and on His chest and on His forehead and in His hands. And He wears the holy mitre on His forehead.

The Scripture says, "Who is he that condemneth? It is Christ that died, yea rather, that is risen again, who is even at the right hand of God, who also maketh intercession for us" (Rom. 8:34). If you were in trouble and you had the best lawyer on the North American continent pleading your cause, don't you suppose you would sleep tonight? Well, you have the best advocate above pleading your cause. And in Philippians, "In nothing be terrified by your adversaries: which is to them an evident token of perdition, but to you of salvation, and that of God" (1:28). Then Ephesians 4:27, "Neither give place to the devil." James 4:7, "Submit yourselves therefore to God. Resist the devil, and he will flee from you."

In the early days of the alliance, here is one song they used to sing: "Jesus is victor, His work is complete, crushing all enemies under His feet. Jesus is victor. He died not in vain. Risen and glorified, Jesus doth rein. Jesus is victor, the battle is won. We can do nothing for all has been done. Jesus is victor, the foe from the dust never can rise again if we but trust."

Simpson wrote, "Fainting soldier of the Lord, Hear His sweet inspiring word—'I have conquered all thy foes, I have suffered all thy woes; Struggling soldier trust in Me, I have overcome for Thee.'" I have overcome; you don't have to overcome anybody nor anything. He is your overcomer. "Fear not, tho' thy foes be strong; Faint not, tho' the strife be long; Trust thy glorious Captain's power, Watch with Him one little hour; Hear Him calling, 'Follow Me, I have overcome for Thee.'"

You can overcome in an overcoming Savior. You don't have to do it yourself. Some of you are trying to. You are trying to push and strain and sweat and get through. When a priest went through to the holy place, they didn't allow him to wear wool, he had to wear linen because the Bible said they didn't want anyone sweating there before the altar. Human perspiration work is not the victory of Christ. It took sweat and tears and blood and dying, and it took victorious resurrection and ascension to bring us the victory. But for you and me, it takes trust, trust in the Lord Jesus.

I don't know whether I have ever been healed, but two or three times in my life, I have had some things happen to me. When you get under the load, and you begin to get down and you pray and you read the Scripture and you can't get above—things are rolling on you, and you are physically down and tired. One day, I got down on my knees and suddenly said, "By a faith imparted to me from heaven, I won't take anymore. God, I have had enough of this. This doesn't come from You. This comes from my enemy, the devil. And I will not take any more." And the burden rolled from me.

I walked along the street in an eastern city one time, heavy with a load on my heart and a burden I could not escape, and it was getting bigger. And one day, when I walked on a street called Elm Street, I suddenly said, "Now, God, no more of this. I won't take it." And snap, the thing left my heart, and I never had it back on me. That is not defying God. That is defying the devil and believing God. And God loves that kind of courage, friend. He loves it.

You don't have to be kicked around. God never meant for you to be a football. He meant for you to humble yourself and be chastened and to let Him do the chastening. But when the devil starts getting funny with you, you dare resist him.

It is time you stop letting the devil push you around. You've met every condition you know. You want God worse than you want to live. And you'd lie down tonight and die if you knew the Lord wanted you to. And God knows it, and worst, the devil knows it. But still, you are wrapped in grave clothes. And you are frightened, and you are timid. And a great chilly fear lies on you. Now it is time you dare to rise and in the sweet faith in Jesus Christ say, "I will not take this any longer, I am a child of God! Why should I go mourning all the day?"

The burden will roll, just as sure as you will live. I know from personal experience. And I have come out of tailspins that I think would have put me in the hospital with a nervous breakdown—pressures of work, exhaustion, and troubles. And then suddenly, I said, "Now, God, I had enough of this." And He said, "Alright, son, I was waiting to hear you say that. I was waiting to hear until you said you had enough. The devil has been kicking you around, and I was just waiting to see how long you'd take it." And off rolls the burden.

THE ABILITY
OF THE CHURCH

*Now about the gifts of the Spirit, brothers
and sisters, I do not want you to be uninformed.*

1 Corinthians 12:1

Anything that God can do through all of His church, He can do through a local church, a local group. These various functions are the abilities to work, and they are called gifts. Paul said, "Having then gifts differing according to the grace that is given to us" (Rom. 12:6a); "Now concerning spiritual gifts, brethren" (1 Cor. 12:1a); "But covet earnestly the best gifts" (12:31a); "When he ascended up on high, he . . . gave gifts unto men" (Eph. 4:8).

So, when the gifts are lodged in the body of Christ, in the local church, they are the ability to do. By way of illustration, your stomach is a gift from God. The purpose of it is not to hold up your trousers, just something to put a belt around. The stomach has a purpose and a function. What is your liver for? What are your eyes for? They have specific purposes and functions, something to do and accomplish. If they do their function and all the others cooperate, you will be a healthy, useful person.

We have these gifts in the church in the same manner. Paul said in his careful instructions in the God-inspired writings that these gifts are placed to get things done. They exist in the church for a purpose.

Now, Paul also used sports to illustrate, so if I use sports to illustrate, don't say I'm not spiritual. I have no ambition to be more spiritual than the apostle Paul! You know that a baseball team in action has nine men. There's a fellow to catch the ball, there's a fellow to pitch the ball, there's a fellow in center field, and there's a fellow on first base and second base, etc. Each man in his own position has a function, and each knows what he is to do. As long as he does his job skillfully, the team as a unit is hard to beat. Whenever a team gets a star who does not care whether the team wins or not, provided he can shine, the success of the team as a winning unit is sacrificed.

Paul says that these gifts are in the body. Some say that there are only nine, because the opening verses of 1 Corinthians lists nine. But do you know that I have counted at least eighteen in the Scriptures? There may be some that overlap, and the list could be reduced to fifteen. Let me follow the Scriptures closely now and staying by the Word of God, let me simply name the gift functions of the divine body that are named by Paul.

First, there is the gift of an apostle, or an ambassador or messenger. There is the gift that makes a prophet. There is the gift that makes a teacher. Then, there is the gift that makes an exhorter. There is the gift that makes the ruler. That would be someone like the old Presbyterians called a ruling elder. Then there are the gifts of wisdom, of knowledge, of faith, of healing. There is a gift of miracles, a gift of tongues, a gift of interpretation, a gift of discernment, a gift of helps, a gift of mercy showing, a gift of government, a gift of liberality, and the gift of the evangelist.

There you have it. These are the gifts that are in the body, the functions that enable the Holy Spirit to work. As long as you have the bodily members, the life within you can find its mode of expression.

As long as your hands are obedient to the head, they will be all right. Just as long as your feet take orders from the head, you will not get hit as you cross the street. Just as long as the members of your body do their work and take orders from the head, you will be all right. Just as long as the church of Christ recognizes the Lord as being the Head of the church, and Christians as members in particular and these members gifted with "abilities to do," we will have a revived and blessed church!

WHEN THE GIFTS ARE MISSING

Remember that the work of the church is done by the Spirit, working through these gifts and through these gifted members. Where these gifts are not present, or not recognized, or denied, the church is thrown back upon other ways of getting a work done.

There are several mistaken emphases in our circles, and the first is just plain humanism. If you had no hands, you would have to do the best you could without hands. If you had no eyes, you would be doing the best you could without eyes. If you had no feet, you would have to crawl around as well as you could without feet. So, if we deny or refuse to recognize that there are members, and that there are gifts in these members, then we are thrown back upon mere humanism. We have this in great measure today. We are thrown back upon talent—just talent. Let me solemnly tell you that the Holy Spirit never works with mere talent. Don't be mistaken by the parable where Jesus uses the word *talent*, which was a sum of money (Matt. 25:14–30). It had no reference to the ability to sing or imitate or project— whatever it is that theatrical people do with their talent.

Our second mistake is that we are thrown back upon psychology as a substitute. I am quite amused and somewhat disgusted with some of my ministerial brethren who are so busy studying psychology in order to know how to handle their congregations. When you have a Bible and a mind, a mouth and the Holy Spirit, why do you have to study psychology? I recall my own experience as a young fellow when I thought it necessary to become a great student of psychology. I studied Watson and James, and particularly Freud, who was the father of psychiatry and psychoanalysis. I learned all the terms and all the pitch. I'm not dumb about psychology, but there is no use bringing psychology to the pulpit when you have the Holy Spirit. If you have the gift of the Spirit, you do not need to study Freud. If you do study him, that is all right, but don't bring him to the pulpit with you!

Another mistake we make is dependence on business methods. I get amused and hurt a little about these brethren and their business methods, trying to carry on the work of God after the fashion of the American businessman. When we carry on the way they do on Madison Avenue or Wall Street, the body is all artificial limbs. It won't work!

Then there is the political technique, with persuasion by sales methods. I think we are going to have to restudy this whole teaching of the place of the Holy Spirit in the church, so the body can operate again. If the life goes out of a man's body, he is said to be a corpse. He is what they call "the remains." It is sad, but humorously sad, that a strong, fine man with shining eyes and vibrant voice, a living man, dies, and we say, "'The remains' can be seen at a funeral home." All the remains of the man, and the least part about him, is what you can see there in the funeral home. The living man is gone. You have only the body. The body is "the remains."

NO LIFE WITHOUT THE SPIRIT

So it is in the church of Christ. It is literally true that some churches are dead. The Holy Spirit has gone out of them and all you have left are "the remains." You have the potential of the church but you do not have the church, just as you have in a dead man the potential of a living man but you do not have a living man. He can't talk, he can't taste, he can't touch, he can't feel, he can't smell, he can't see, he can't hear—because he is dead! The soul has gone out of the man, and when the Holy Spirit is not present in the church, you have to get along after the methods of business or politics or psychology or human effort.

You cannot overstate the necessity for the Holy Spirit in the church, if you say it according to the Scriptures, for without the Spirit there can be nothing done for eternity. Someone will say, "If that's true, why don't we just cast our lot in with the tongues movement, because they believe you can be sure you are filled with the Spirit, but you must have the evidence of tongues?"

Well, in answer, I have known and studied these dear brethren, and I have preached to them for a long, long time. I have studied them, and I know them very well, and I am very sympathetic with them. There are some churches that are very sane and very beautiful and godly. I don't want to hurt anyone's feelings, but it is true that, as Christians, we have to smile and thank God for the truth, whether it hurts or not. The movement itself has magnified one single gift above all others, and that one gift is the one Paul said was the least. An unscriptural exhibition of that gift results, and there is a tendency to place personal feeling above the Scriptures, and we must never, never do that!

God has given us the Book, brother, and the Book comes first. If it can't be shown in the Book, then I don't want anyone coming to me all aquiver and trying to tell me anything. The Book—you must give me the Word!

Another direction of teaching in our day is this: Some brethren say that the gifts of the Spirit ceased when the apostles died. With the death of the apostles, there are no gifts of the Spirit, they declare.

Now, here we have two directions: The first teaching that before you can be sure you are filled with the Spirit you must have the evidence of tongues; the other, that in these days all gifts are canceled and dead and not available in the church.

EXAMPLES FROM HISTORY

How are we going to find our way around in all this? Let me remind you of certain people who lived and served God and some of the things they did. Let us see how either of these two extremes answer these exploits for God.

Take Augustine, for instance, the bishop of Hippo, that saintly man who walked with God and wrote a great confession of faith. There is more of God in Augustine's *Confessions* than there is in all of the books written in fundamental circles in the last fifty years. If I were on an island and I could have a pile of all the fundamental, full-gospel literature written in the last fifty years, or have Augustine's *Confessions*, I would give up all the rest to keep the one book because God is in that book! He's the man who was a great orator and a great student of Greek oratory. When he was filled with the Holy Spirit, he said, "I lost my taste for Greek oratory and it bothered me. Later on I discovered why. I found not Christ in the Greek orator." He was one of the six great brains of all times, and he gave it all up that he might follow Christ.

Consider Bernard of Cluny, also. Bernard of Cluny was a saint, and he wrote Jerusalem the Golden. You remember that great thing, "Jerusalem, the golden, with milk and honey blest." This man walked with God. He had a twin, Bernard of Clairvaux, who wrote, "Jesus, the very thought of Thee with sweetness fills my breast" and other such beautiful and wonderful hymns.

Then there was Richard Rolle, who lived in the fourteenth century. He was a monk, but he got so blessed he couldn't stay in the monastery, so he got himself a guitar and went all over England preaching the gospel he called "Heat, fragrance and song." It was hot, it was sweet, and it was music.

There was Brother Lawrence, the man who practiced the presence of God. He wouldn't pick up a straw from the ground but for the love of God. When he was dying, they said, "What are you doing, Brother Lawrence?" He said, "I'm doing what I plan to do through all eternity—worship God. When I die I won't change my occupation. I have just been worshiping God for forty years on earth, and when I get to heaven I'll just keep right on doing what I am doing."

Recall, too, Thomas à Kempis who wrote *The Imitation of Christ*, and that man they called Dr. Martin Luther, who said, "I'm going to get married to tease the pope and to make the devil mad." He was the man who stood and said, "If every tile on the housetop was a devil, here I stand. I can do nothing else, so help me God!" He gave the Word of God back to the church and put the pope in his place.

Zinzendorf was that rich German nobleman who saw a painting of Christ crucified on the cross. He wept and said, "If He died for me, I must give myself to Him!" Out of his devotion and vision came the emphasis from which all of the great missionary movements of the present day have sprung.

There was Tersteegen, a silk weaver in Germany who had such an experience with God that he signed a covenant with God in his own blood. His cottage became a center of spiritual power for all of Germany.

John Newton wrote "How Sweet the Name of Jesus Sounds." This wonderful man was a slave of slaves in Africa and yet was converted and became one of the most blazing saints of his generation.

How would we get along without the works of Charles Wesley? His "Jesus, Lover of My Soul," "Love Divine, All Loves Excelling," and his "And Can It Be That I Should Gain an Interest in the Saviour's Blood?" are just a few. And his brother, John

Wesley, the man who was an egg catcher, for they threw barrels of eggs at him, you know! He went right on preaching until he changed the whole moral complexion of England. The historians said that he saved England from a revolution.

Consider William Booth, who started the Salvation Army, or Jonathan Edwards, the great American preacher who brought the great revival—a great awakening. Think of Frederick Faber, who wrote "Oh, Jesus, Jesus, dearest Lord, forgive me if I say, for very love, Thy sacred Name a thousand times a day"; and Reginald Heber, the Anglican, who wrote "Holy, Holy, Holy, Lord God Almighty."

In our own country there was Charles Finney, the lawyer who was converted and filled with the Holy Spirit, so that he said, "The Holy Spirit descended upon me in a manner that seemed to go through me, body and soul. I could feel the impression like a wave of electricity, going through and through me. Indeed, it seemed to come in waves and waves of liquid love. . . . like the very breath of God. . . . it seemed to fan me like immense wings." Recall with me David Livingstone, who opened Africa to the gospel; and Charles Spurgeon, who preached to six thousand persons in London every Sunday for a lifetime. It was said of Spurgeon that his prayers healed more sick people in London than all the doctors put together.

George Mueller went to England and opened an orphanage at Bristol. This man prayed down millions of dollars into his hands and blessed thousands of people and brought up thousands of orphans, and God never refused him anything. Think of Frances Havergal, of whom it was said that when she came into a room, there was a consciousness of two people coming into the room—Frances Havergal and the Holy Spirit.

Evan Roberts was the man who prayed, "Bend me, oh God, bend me!" and God bent him and gave Wales its great revival. Dr. Seng, the Chinese Christian who was beaten and sewed in a sack and bruised and kicked about, went out and preached up and down China, and God came on him with great miracles and wonders.

Dr. A. B. Simpson started out with eight people who prayed for missions, and now we remember him as the founder of the sixth largest missionary society in the world.

Billy Nicholson, dear old Billy, who went to be with his Lord not so very long ago, was the evangelist who came to Ireland at a time of political unrest and moral decadence. So many people were converted under Billy Nicholson that a revolution was avoided.

Did you ever hear of the Irish-Canadian woman who was called Holy Ann? They said Holy Ann talked about her Father so intimately that you would think that God had no other children but her.

Have you read the life of Sammy Morris? I never saw Sammy Morris myself, but I once stood with bared head beside his grave. Sammy Morris, the Kru boy from Africa, who heard about the Holy Spirit and came to the United States. He worked his way here to talk to somebody who could tell him about the Holy Spirit. Someone took him around New York City and said, "Look at this building, look at that building." Sammy Morris broke in and said, "I haven't come to New York to look at buildings. Do you know anything about the Holy Spirit?" He went on to Taylor University and said, "I understand you Methodists believe in the Holy Spirit, and I want to know more about Him. If you have a room anywhere up under the edge of the roof that no other student will take, that's the one I want." Sammy Morris, a reflection of Christ, lived only a short time. He lies buried in the city of Fort Wayne, Indiana, where I stood beside his grave.

I can name only a few—reams of paper would have to be used to write just the names of the great saints who have lived and have rocked and shaken nations and have cleaned up cities and towns. Revivals now come and go and leave the communities unchanged. Revivals in those days left the imprint of God.

HOW DID THEY DO IT?

Now, for those who say that the gifts died with the apostles: If the gifts of the Spirit died with the apostles, how did Augustine, Bernard of Cluny, Richard Rolle, Brother Lawrence, Thomas à Kempis, Luther, Zinzendorf, Tersteegen, William Booth, Jonathan Edwards, Charles Finney, Charles Spurgeon, George Mueller, A.B. Simpson, Billy Nicholson, Holy Ann, and Sammy Morris perform the works of God? How did they do it? If the Holy Spirit has no gifts for men, did they do it by their intellect, did they do it by their brains? No, my brethren, these were men and women of gifts, and the gifts were in them, and the Spirit of God used them mightily, working through them as my soul works through my hands.

On the other side, if we are not filled with the Spirit unless we have the evidence of tongues, then Augustine, Bernard, Thomas à Kempis, Frederick Faber, Charles Finney, David Livingstone, Charles Spurgeon, and George Mueller weren't filled with the Holy Spirit. Not one of them ever said anything about the evidence of tongues. Can we say they wrought their mighty, world-changing deeds in the power of the flesh? Oh no, brother! I don't go along with either extreme. I know that the gifts of the Spirit did not die with the apostles. I know that there are gifts today in the Christian church, even in some churches that don't know they have them.

We cannot help ourselves by going somewhere else or joining something new. Brother, you don't get help by going out somewhere and "joining" something. God is not looking for tags or titles or names! He is looking for people. He is looking for loving, humble, clean people, and if He can find such people, He is prepared to move in at once with great power.

"But ye shall receive power" (Acts 1:8). "But covet earnestly the best gifts" (1 Cor. 12:31). Anything that God has ever done for a soul He will do for anyone else, if the conditions are met. The Lord who blessed these men that I spoke about, and the thousands who followed them but whose names are not known, is willing to do the same for us as He did for them.

FAITH OR UNBELIEF

Unbelief says, "Some other time, but not now; some other place, but not here; some other people, but not us." Faith says, "Anything He did anywhere else He will do here; anything He did any other time He is willing to do now; anything He ever did for other people He is willing to do for us!" With our feet on the ground and our head cool but with our heart ablaze with the love of God, we walk out in this fullness of the Spirit, if we will yield and obey. God wants to work through you!

The Counselor has come, and He doesn't care about the limits of locality, geography, time, or nationality. The body of Christ is bigger than all of these. The question is: Will you open your heart?

When Noah sent forth the dove, and she could find no place to land, he "put forth his hand, and took her, and pulled her in unto him into the ark" (Gen. 8:9). If I could fall back on that little illustration, would you reach out your hand by faith and pull the Holy Spirit in unto you? It would make a great and wonderful difference in your life. I've seen it happen and there's no reason why it can't happen for you if you fully obey.

THE PURPOSE
OF THE CHURCH

Ascribe to the LORD the glory due his name;
worship the LORD in the splendor of his holiness.

PSALM 29:2

Why did Christ come? Why was He conceived? Why was He born? Why was He crucified? Why did He rise again? Why is He now at the right hand of the Father?

The answer to all these questions is, "In order that He might make worshipers out of rebels; in order that He might restore us again to the place of worship we knew when we were first created."

Now because we were created to worship, worship is the normal employment of moral beings. It's the normal employment, not something stuck on or added, like listening to a concert or admiring flowers. It is something that is built into human nature. Every glimpse of heaven shows them worshiping. Ezekiel 1:1–5: the creatures out of the fire were worshiping God. Isaiah

6:1–6: we see the Lord high and lifted up and hear the creatures saying, "Holy, holy, holy, is the LORD of hosts." Revelation 4:8–11: God opens heaven and we see them there worshiping God the Father. And in 5:6–14, we see them worshiping God the Son.

Worship is a moral imperative. In Luke 19:37–40 the whole multitude of disciples were worshiping the Lord as He came along and some rebuked them. The Lord said, "Don't rebuke them; if they didn't worship Me the stones would cry out."

Now, worship is the missing jewel in modern evangelicalism. We're organized; we work; we have our agendas.

We have almost everything, but there's one thing that the churches, even the gospel churches, do not have: that is the ability to worship. We are not cultivating the art of worship. It's the one shining gem that is lost to the modern church, and I believe that we ought to search for this until we find it.

WHAT WORSHIP IS

I think I ought to talk a little more about what worship is and what it would be like if it were in the church.

Well, it's an attitude, a state of mind, a sustained act, subject to degrees of perfection and intensity. As soon as He sends the Spirit of His Son into our hearts, we say "Abba" and we're worshiping. That's one thing. But it's quite another thing to be worshipers in the full New Testament sense of the word.

Now I say that worship is subject to degrees of perfection and intensity. There have been those who worshiped God to the point where they were in ecstasies of worship. I once saw a man kneel at an altar, taking Communion. Suddenly he broke into holy laughter. This man laughed until he wrapped his arms around himself as if he was afraid he would burst just out of sheer delight in the presence of Almighty God. A few times I have seen other people rapt in an ecstasy of worship where they were carried away with it, and I have also heard some simplehearted new converts saying "Abba Father." So worship is capable of running from the very simple to the most intense and sublime.

THE ELEMENTS OF WORSHIP

Now what are the factors that you will find present in worship? Let me give you a few of them as I go along.

First, there is *boundless confidence*. You cannot worship a Being you cannot trust. Confidence is necessary to respect, and respect is necessary to worship. Worship rises or falls in any church altogether depending upon the attitude we take toward God, whether we see God big or whether we see Him little. Most of us see God too small; our God is too little. David said, "O magnify the LORD with me" (Ps. 34:3), and "magnify" doesn't mean to make God big. You can't make God big. But you can see Him big.

Worship, I say, rises or falls with our concept of God; that is why I do not believe in these half-converted cowboys who call God the Man Upstairs. I do not think they worship at all because their concept of God is unworthy of God and unworthy of them. And if there is one terrible disease in the church of Christ, it is that we do not see God as great as He is. We're too familiar with God.

Communion with God is one thing; familiarity with God is

quite another thing. I don't even like—and this may hurt some of your feelings, but they'll heal—to hear God called "You." "You" is a colloquial expression. I can call a man "you," but I ought to call God "Thou" and "Thee." Now, I know these are old Elizabethan words, but I also know that there are some things too precious to cast lightly away and I think that when we talk to God we ought to use the pure, respectful pronouns.

Also I think we ought not to talk too much about Jesus just as Jesus. I think we ought to remember who He is. "He is thy Lord; and worship thou him" (Ps. 45:11). And though He comes down to the lowest point of our need and makes Himself accessible to us as tenderly as a mother to her child, still don't forget that when John saw Him—that John who had lain on His bosom—he fell at His feet as dead.

I've heard all kinds of preachers. I've heard the ignorant boasters; I've heard the dull, dry ones; I've heard the eloquent ones; but the ones who have helped me most were the ones who were awestruck in the presence of the God about whom they spoke. They might have a sense of humor, they might be jovial; but when they talked about God another tone came into their voice altogether; this was something else, something wonderful. I believe we ought to have again the old biblical concept of God that makes God awful and makes men lie face down and cry, "Holy, holy, holy, LORD God Almighty." That would do more for the church than everything or anything else.

Then there is *admiration*—that is, appreciation of the excellency of God. Man is better qualified to appreciate God than any other creature because he was made in His image and is the only creature who was. This admiration for God grows and grows until it fills the heart with wonder and delight. "In our astonished reverence we confess Thine uncreated loveliness," said the hymn writer. "In our astonished reverence." The God of the modern evangelical rarely astonishes anybody. He manages to stay pretty much within the Constitution. Never breaks over our bylaws. He's a very well-behaved God and very denominational and very much one of us, and we ask Him to help us when we're in trouble and look to Him to watch over us when we're asleep. The God of the modern evangelical isn't a God I could have much respect for. But when the Holy Ghost shows us God as He is we admire Him to the point of wonder and delight.

Fascination is another element in true worship. To be filled with moral excitement. To be captivated and charmed and entranced. Excited, not with how big you're getting or how big the offering was. Not with how many people came out to church. But entranced with who God is, and struck with astonished wonder at the inconceivable elevation and magnitude and splendor of Almighty God.

I remember as a young Christian when I got my first awful, wonderful, entrancing vision of God. I was in West Virginia in the woods sitting on a log reading the Scriptures along with an old Irish evangelist by the name of Robert J. Cunningham, now long in heaven. I got up and wandered away to have prayer by myself. I had been reading one of the driest passages imaginable from the Scriptures—where Israel came out of Egypt and God arranged them into a diamond-shaped camp. He put Levi in the middle and Reuben out in front and Benjamin behind. It was a diamond-shaped moving city with a flame of fire in the middle giving light. Suddenly, it broke over me: God is a geometrician;

He's an artist! When He laid out that city, He laid it out skillfully, diamond-shaped with a plume in the middle, and it suddenly swept over me like a wave of the sea: How beautiful God is and how artistic and how poetic and how musical, and I worshiped God there under that tree all by myself. You know, after that I began to love the old hymns and I have been a lover of the great hymns ever since.

Next is *adoration*, to love God with all the power within us. To love God with fear and wonder and yearning and awe. To yearn for God with great yearning, and to love Him to a point where it is both painful and delightful. At times, this will lead us to breathless silence. I think that some of the greatest prayer is prayer where you don't say one single word or ask for anything. Now God does answer and He does give us what we ask for. That's plain; nobody can deny that unless he denies the Scriptures. But that's only one aspect of prayer, and it's not even the important aspect. Sometimes I go to God and say, "God, if Thou dost never answer another prayer while I live on this earth, I will still worship Thee as long as I live and in the ages to come for what Thou hast done already." God's already put me so far in debt that if I were to live one million millenniums I couldn't pay Him for what He's done for me.

We go to God as we send a boy to a grocery store with a long written list, "God, give me this, give me this, and give me this," and our gracious God often does give us what we want. But I think God is disappointed because we make Him to be no more than a source of what we want. Even our Lord Jesus is presented too often as "Someone who will meet your need." That's the throbbing heart of modern evangelism. You're in need and Jesus will meet your need. He's the Need-meeter. Well, He is that indeed; but, ah, He's infinitely more than that.

Now when the mental and emotional and spiritual factors that I've spoken to you about are present and, as I've admitted, in varying degrees of intensity, in song, in praise, in prayer, and in mental prayer, you are worshiping. Do you know what mental prayer is? I mean by that, do you know what it is to pray continually? Old Brother Lawrence, who wrote *The Practice of the Presence of God*, said, "If I'm washing dishes I do it to the glory of God and if I pick up a straw from the ground I do it to the glory of God. I'm in communion with God all the time." He said, "The rules tell me that I have to take time off to go alone to pray, and I do, but such times do not differ any from my regular communion." He had learned the art of fellowship with God, continuous and unbroken.

I am afraid of the pastor who enters the pulpit as a different person from what he was before. Reverend, you should never think a thought or do a deed or be caught in any situation that you couldn't carry into the pulpit with you without embarrassment. You should never have to be a different man or get a new voice and a new sense of solemnity when you enter the pulpit. You should be able to enter the pulpit with the same spirit and the same sense of reverence that you had just before when you were talking to someone about the common affairs of life. Moses came down from the mount to speak to the people. Woe be to the church when the pastor comes up to the pulpit or comes into the pulpit! He must come down to the pulpit always. Wesley, they said, habitually dwelt with God but came down at times to speak to the people. So should it be with all of us. *Amen.*

THE SERVICE
OF THE CHURCH

Religion that God our Father accepts as pure and faultless
is this: to look after orphans and widows in their distress
and to keep oneself from being polluted by the world.

James 1:27

The church is here to serve. It is not here to play. And I begin by saying that the church serves only as its members serve. Even the most democratic-minded Christian is being influenced, and so led to some degree, by some other Christian living or dead. He cannot escape it; that is the way he is made and he might as well accept it.

I suppose I am three-quarters Baptist. I don't know. Baptists say I am, but I can't quite follow along with what I've heard in some quarters that there is such a thing as a mystic and invisible church. The church is composed of people. If, as they say, the simplest form of a local church is "where two or three are gathered together in my name, there am I in the midst of them"

(Matt. 18:20), then I accept that as being a factual statement.

But if this is true and you take away the two or three, you don't have any church. And those two or three have names. They are people. They have telephone numbers, social security numbers, and they weigh so much, they look a certain way, they are people. And the church is composed of people. And if you take the people away, there isn't any ghostly, mystical church hovering around waiting to be embodied. The church is people. And we try to dodge out from under our personal responsibilities sometimes by saying, "The great church is serving." The great church doesn't exist. The great mystical church is a figment of human imagination. The church might not always be identified, but wherever she is, she's people.

If there are no church people there, there's no church. If there are church people, there are individuals. Keep that in mind. Even the Holy Ghost said there were about 120 in that upper chamber. And when the Spirit of God came to bring the church into being, there were about 120. They were individuals, and they named some of them.

So, the church is composed of people, and if the church is going to serve as I have previously declared it should, then it can serve only as its members serve. The Holy Spirit is the central nervous system of the church, you know. And He can work only as He gets the obedience of His members. He can work only as He has the intelligent, Bible-taught cooperation of his members. The failure of the members is the failure of the total church. As the individual members serve, the church is automatically serving. The church is serving where they serve. The church is witnessing as and where they witness. The church and the individual members are one and the same thing. You cannot take away the people and still have the church. The church takes two: Jesus Christ in the midst, and people in whose midst He is.

ACTING LIKE THE WORLD

Now, a lot of churches don't know why they are here. We don't know why we are here. I scan a good many magazines. I rarely read them, but I scan them. And if I see a good article, I'll read it. But I learned from the brethren who were writing the articles that we don't know why we are here. We are dressed up and have nowhere to go and nothing to do. We are not sure of ourselves. The result is that the churches are looking around to see what others are doing, and then they are copying what others are doing and do it, as they say, for Jesus' sake. No matter what is done, the church picks it up and brushes it off and dips it in holy water and says, "Now, we're doing it for Jesus' sake, and it's alright. The world is doing it for the world, but we are doing it for Jesus." The point is they're doing the same thing. And if that little striped animal out in the woods was around your house, you couldn't make him any more desirable by saying that he was there for Jesus' sake. He's still what he is, and you can't change him by putting a holy name on him. So, as long as the church does what the world does, the church is worldly.

I received two pieces of mail. They came the same day. And one of them is from the Kenosha Cornhuskers, and they want to put on a social for us at our church, to raise money. I don't want to be satirical nor unkind. The mail includes a picture of a fellow with a cowboy suit on and a guitar. I like him. He looks nice. And if I met him, I'd like him, and I'm sure he'd like me. And I'd be friendly to him and good to him. But because the church doesn't know what she is called to do, people from the outside look in and suggest things. . . . And lots of churches take this up. They don't know what they are called to do. They haven't the remotest idea, so if someone suggests they have a bunny hop and learn all the grips, they learn them. And get a little extra and put it in the kitty for the pastor's salary and for what they call benevolences.

Well, it's a lack of information, a lack of instruction. I hope you won't think I am bitter about this.

Consider:

Now there were in the church that was at Antioch certain prophets and teachers; as Barnabas, and Simeon that was called Niger, and Lucius of Cyrene, and Manaen, which had been brought up with Herod the tetrarch, and Saul.

As they ministered to the Lord, and fasted, the Holy Ghost said, Separate me Barnabas and Saul for the work whereunto I have called them.

And when they had fasted and prayed, and laid their hands on them, they sent them away.

So they, being sent forth by the Holy Ghost, departed unto Seleucia; and from thence they sailed to Cyprus. (Acts 13:1–4)

Now if the churches were doing this, would any Kenosha Cornhusker boys write to them, "Can we come in and play and put on a show?" They wouldn't. They'd stand in respect. If it could be said of all other churches as it was said of them in Solomon's porch—they were all together in Solomon's porch and no man durst join himself to them (Acts 5:12–13). They were a holy people. The flame was still on their fork and the scent of another world was on them. And nobody was going to suggest that they ring the cowbell and sing "Old MacDonald Had a Farm," a harmless thing. And if anybody wants to do it, I repeat, I occasionally turn the radio on and hear someone sing "Old MacDonald," and I don't mind it. But that is not the church. That is not what we are called to do. That is not why we are here. That is not our business. That is not our job. That isn't the world we live in. We live in another world, an elevated world, a world of another kind altogether.

The second piece of mail shows that if you take a biblical direction and stick to it, it pays off. This mail came from a missionary mother, not of the Alliance, but from the Newfoundland and Labrador Outpost Mission in Happy Valley, Labrador. This lady wrote,

Dear Brother Tozer, greetings in Christ's name. On the afternoon of December 24, my youngest son Daniel was suddenly thrust into eternity as the missionary plane which he was piloting was caught in a white-out en route to Happy Valley from North West River where he had flown earlier that morning to carry Christmas mail and parcels to hospital patients and children at the Grenfell Missions School. Just before leaving home at 1:30 that afternoon, he read a sermon by you titled, "A Process of Becoming" in the December issue of Pentecostal Evangel, perhaps the last words he read before entering eternity. While working at United Airlines in Chicago, in '56 and '57, in preparation for his ministry up here, he often attended your church and told me that he received more spiritual food [there] than in any other church he ever attended. Thus, when the magazine came in the mail, he eagerly read your sermon, and I am sure it was a grand climax in preparation for death which was to meet him a few hours later.

He is in heaven now.

I don't know him. He was evidently one of the students that comes and goes. But Brother McAfee helped him to learn to love a great hymn. And instead of MacDonald's Farm, McAfee lead him singing the great hymns of Watts and Wesley and Montgomery and Faber. And instead of the bunny hop, I seriously taught the great truths of God. And that young man warmed up to it and became a missionary. And when he saw my name, he read my sermon. He got into his plane and said, "I'll see you at sundown." But he never saw a sundown. A snowstorm brought him down.

What are we called to do? Are we called to play the harmless play? Are we called to put on nice heels, even the harmless ones? Or are we called seriously to pray and to live and to teach and to witness and to worship and to sing and to create or have God create about us an atmosphere where a young, serious-minded student can walk in and say, "I never got so much help in all my life?" And it was a Pentecostal boy, remember. "Never got so much help in all my life." Then go away to die in a snowstorm taking food and medicine to babies! . . .

God bless the Cornhuskers and love them. I'd like to pray with them and talk with them and give them a New Testament. I don't dislike them. I just say they don't know who we are. They are judging us by what they've seen, and it is not their fault. It is the great church's fault. They are judging us by what they've seen in other churches, not all others, but churches.

OUR COMMISSION

A solemn commission is laid upon us as individuals. If we wait for concerted actions—that is, everybody—we'll never get anything done. There is always somebody who has to rise and do something—always someone alone, then another and another. But if we wait for any theoretical, concerted action, nobody will get anything done.

I'd like to point out that we can serve no generation but this one. Yesterday's generation is gone. Tomorrow's generation has not been born. But today, all around us is our own generation. This is the big day of our opportunity. And we are called to practical service.

I have emphasized, as every true Bible teacher ought to do, that the beating heart of the church is the fullness of the Holy Ghost, the presence of Christ, worship, and love. That is the beating heart of the church, but that is not all. You haven't discharged your obligation when you've come here on a Sunday morning and sung a Watt's hymn and read the Scripture together and listened to an exhortation and made your offering. You haven't discharged your obligation. That is only the Sunday worship.

John Ruskin, the great English art critique and philosopher and Christian, seriously questioned whether we ought to call this "service" at all. You go and sing a song, and read the Scripture and enjoy yourself and have fellowship with happy people in the church. That is service? We call that Christian service. He doubted that that is service. Well I don't doubt, I think it is. It is the heart of the church. It is to the work of the church what your engine is to your car. I think it is to the work of the church what your heart is to your body. It is the throbbing, vibrating center of it all. And that religious group that tries to work without worshiping will soon be doing the devil's work. We've got to be worshipers first in order that we might be workers.

We work out of our worship, but there is always a danger in everything. Don't forget it. The holier our worship is, the more dangerous it is. And the further into the throne of God it is, the more temptations the devil throws around it. So, all this I'm talking about—worshiping and having the Lord and the Holy Ghost here and standing by the cause of missions and putting our hands on men and women and sending them out to all parts of the world to preach the gospel—that is so important, my friends! But even that can become a source of temptation. Don't forget there are other sorts of service too.

Jesus did it. He went around doing good, and we are called to practical service. Not only the beautiful things—worship and song and prayer and teaching—but feeding, and clothing and helping and praying and scrubbing and cooking and peace-making and all these things that we are supposed to do as Christians.

Living under the circumstances you do and living on the high level you live, you ought to have somebody in Korea, Austria, or somewhere whom you are feeding—at least one person in addition to supporting your missions and your church, and paying your taxes. Woe to us that we live in a favored land like America: We eat ourselves into obesity and early heart attack and dainty feet never touch a bare floor. And then they are hungry from birth to death in many parts of the world.

I believe it is the business of the church to serve. I think that when we fundamentalists and evangelicals forgot that we were called to feed the poor and give a cup of cold water to the one who is in need, I think we forgot something very wonderful.

Dr. Walter Wilson's brother, Dyke Wilson, writes to me sometimes. I don't know much about him. I only know that he is a very brilliant and very wonderful Christian man. He wrote me and sent me an ondograph sermon. It was a plea that God's church might serve God's people, that we might serve the poor and the needy.

Now, brethren, let us fight to escape the trap. We are well-fed, well-dressed, respectable, cultured—and yet the very poor are afraid to enter our doors. We say we are going where the people are, and I suppose that is right. I'd like to tell you that if it could be done and arranged, I wouldn't mind if one half of my congregation was of another race than mine. I'd preach to Indians and Mexicans and Filipinos and Blacks with the greatest delight. Yet we are moving to another part of the city, and why? Not because we won't, but because our friends won't. They move in and don't want integrated churches like this, so we are going to sell this one to them, bid them Godspeed, and move out. But I hope the day will never be when we are a typical, urban church, birds singing in bushes by our lovely church, and the lawn stretching away. Nobody of any color near us or any other tongue or language, and we will be the typical American, main street, bourgeois Christians without any knowledge of the suffering and the groans of others.

If I thought my church would ever fall into that trap, I'd rather offer my service as assistant superintendent of a rescue mission and bathe the sores of bums off the street. I am not fitted, not trained. I don't run in that direction. I have a ministry that is wider than that, so I am not going to do it. But I will say that if we ever settle down to a smooth, lovely suburban church judging by the length of the cars out in front, I'd take a job with a mission. And I'd lead a drunken woman up the street and sit her in a seat and preach the gospel to her. And I'd rather do it.

Jesus the Christ of God had nowhere to lay His head. And His people suffered and went about in goat skins and sheep skins and did the best they could. They died, not dramatically as they die in movies and shows, but died hungry and weak and bruised and beaten, died before the fire and the lion for Christ's sake. . . .

Jesus served His generation by the will of God. So let's fight to escape the trap of well-fed, well-housed, well-transported American bourgeois Christianity. Let us serve. He served His generation by the will of God, served as He could, served as He knew how. Paul came to serve as he could. Jesus came to serve the way He could. We will serve it as we can. Let us gaze and gaze upon Jesus.

The artists have made the picture of the cross so beautiful that we want to stand and gaze. But I say unto you, nobody ever gazed upon a man dying on a cross with pleasure, nobody but a sadist. For the man dying on the cross: tongue hung out, and he couldn't get it back in after a few hours; jaw drooped, eyes bulged, and blood dripped everywhere. Finally the cold blue came around his mouth to show that he was dying. And instead of noble words being spoken from that cross, the hoarse whisper came through a dry throat.

You and I are called to bear the cross, my brethren. We are called to witness to that kind of Savior. We are not called to be the Dale Carnegie, Norman Vincent Peale, chairman-of-the-board Christianity, but a cross-carrying, Christ-loving, people-loving, serving church. That is what we are called to do. Are you with me?

13

THE WITNESS
OF THE CHURCH

*Therefore go and make disciples of all nations,
baptizing them in the name of the Father and
of the Son and of the Holy Spirit.*

<small>MATTHEW 28:19</small>

The mission of the church is to declare, to proclaim, to witness. She has been left on earth to be a witness to certain great eternal truths that she received from God and that the world could not possibly know unless she told it.

"Go ye therefore, and teach all nations" (Matt. 28:19), said Jesus to the infant church. The church was to teach, and the world was to listen, and all who received the witness of the church were to be baptized and taught further in the mysteries of the kingdom of God.

That was the order established by the new-risen Christ. Those first Christians had seen and heard such wonders as had first terrified them, then filled them with a high spiritual excitement that they could not contain. With joy they turned their backs on the open tomb from which their Lord had walked forth, and literally raced away to spread the news.

A few days later the Holy Spirit came upon them to confirm the truth and to add a new afflatus of moral power to their testimony.

That is how it all began. The early church had the message; the world had only the need for that message. The disciples had seen and touched and handled that Eternal Life, which was with the Father and was manifested unto men; and driven by an irresistible compulsion they went forth to Jew and Greek, bondman and freeman, high and low, to tell, to witness, to declare, to testify. Succeeding generations of Christians, not having seen Christ with their mortal eyes but having met Him in living encounter and having known and experienced Him by the inward operation of the Holy Spirit, told forth the message with the same zeal as had the original band. They had something to tell the world. They were witnesses eagerly testifying. They were devotees and zealots, convinced that they had the truth the world needed desperately and that it could not afford to ignore.

It has been so wherever the church has had eyesight and hearing. When she has been conscious of One walking among the golden candlesticks with a voice like the sound of many waters, she has stood to echo that voice and the world has had to listen. Sometimes, that world turned its back upon its benefactors and persecuted them unto death. Sometimes, it listened as Herod listened to John the Baptist, deeply touched by what it heard but unwilling to obey. Sometimes, it listened sympathetically and numbers of people repented and went on to follow Christ. *But always the world was on the receiving end. The church spake, and the world heard.* Thus it was as Christ said it must be.

A TRAGIC REVERSAL

But hear, O ye heavens, and be astonished, O earth, for a mighty derangement has occurred in the relative position of the church and the world, a transposition so radical and so grotesque as would not have been believed if it had been foretold but a few years ago.

The church has lost her testimony. She has no longer anything to say to the world. Her once robust shout of assurance has faded away to an apologetic whisper. She who one time went out to declare now goes out to inquire. Her dogmatic declaration has become a respectful suggestion, a word of religious advice, given with the understanding that it is after all only an opinion and not meant to sound bigoted.

Not only has the church nothing to say to the world, but the tables have also actually been turned and the ministers of Christ are now going to the world for light. They sit at Adam's feet for instruction and clear their message with the wise and the prudent before they dare deliver it. But the certainty that comes from seeing and the assurance that springs from hearing—where are they?

But let us be more specific. About whom am I speaking here? The liberal who denies the authenticity of the Scriptures? I wish it were so. No, I write off the liberal as long dead and expect nothing from him. It is of the evangelical church that I speak, and of the so-called gospel churches. I speak of the theology of popular evangelism that quotes the Bible copiously but without one trace of authority, accepts the world at its own estimate, chides sinners like a weak-chinned father of a family who has long ago lost control of his household and doesn't expect to be obeyed, offers Christ as a religious tranquilizer who is without sovereignty and without any semblance of Lordship, adopts the world's methods, courts the favor of rich men, politicians, and playboys—with the understanding, of course, that the said playboy will stoop to say a nice word about Jesus now and then.

I refer to a religious journalism ostensibly orthodox but that can scarcely be told in appearance, tone, spirit, language, method, or aim from the secular magazine it so sedulously apes. I refer to the Christianity that says to Christ, "We will eat our own bread, and wear our own apparel: only let us be called by thy name, to take away our reproach" (Isa. 4:1). I refer to the masses of Christians who have "accepted" Jesus, but who turn their churches into playhouses, are entirely ignorant of worship, misunderstand the cross, and are totally blind to the serious implications of discipleship.

Again I refer to the new crop of borderline liberals who use the language of orthodoxy but are nevertheless fellow travelers with old-line liberals and who seek to escape the reproach of the cross by what they like to believe is a dazzling display of intellectualism.

The church is in her Babylonian captivity, and as Israel could not sing the songs of Zion in a strange land, so Christians in bondage have no authoritative message to declare. They must wait for the news broadcast for a text and read *TIME* magazine for a subject. Like the harried editor of a daily newspaper who languishes for a good story when no convenient murder or accident has happened for the last few hours, so the prophet in Babylon waits for a war, a new development in the Middle East, or a space exploit to rescue him from enforced silence and give him a new lease on his pulpit.

RECOVER THE MESSAGE

But what is the church called to declare? What are the hard, bold, everlasting words she has been sent to give to the world?

The first is that God is all in all. He is the great Reality that gives meaning to all other realities.

> Ye are my witnesses, saith the LORD, and my servant whom I have chosen: that ye may know and believe me, and understand that I am he: before me there was no God formed, neither shall there be after me. . . .
>
> Yea, before the day was I am he; and there is none that can deliver out of my hand: I will work, and who shall let it? (Isa. 43:10, 13)

The next great fact is that we are made *by* God and *for* Him. The answer to the question, "Where did I come from?" is never better answered than by the mother who says, "God made you." The pooled knowledge of the world cannot improve upon this simple answer. Scientific research has probed deep into the secrets of how matter operates, but the *origin* of matter lies in deep silence and refuses to give an answer to any questions. God made the heaven and the earth and man upon the earth and He made man for Himself, and there is no other answer to the inquiry, "Why did God make me?"

The Christian is not sent to argue or persuade, nor is he sent to prove or demonstrate; he is sent to declare. "Thus saith the Lord." When he has done this, he makes God responsible for the outcome. No one knows enough and no one can know enough to go beyond this. God made us for Himself: that is the first and last thing that can be said about human existence and whatever more we add is but commentary.

Seeing who God is and who we are, a right relationship between God and us is of vital importance. That God should be glorified in us is so critically important that it stands in lonely grandeur, a moral imperative more compelling than any other that the human heart can acknowledge. To bring ourselves into a place where God will be eternally pleased with us should be the first responsible act of every man.

Knowing our sin and moral ignorance, the impossibility of effecting such a happy relationship becomes instantly evident. Since we cannot go to God, what then shall we do? The answer is found in the Christian witness: it is that God came to us in the Incarnation. "Who is Jesus?" asks the world, and the church answers, "Jesus is God come to us." He is come to seek us, to woo us, to win us to God again. And to do this He needed to die for us redemptively. He must in the same manner undo our sins, destroy our record of sins committed, and break the power of sins entrenched within us. All this, says the Christian witness, He did upon the cross perfectly, effectually, and for good.

"Where is Jesus now?" asks the world, and the Christian answers, "At the right hand of God." He died but He is not dead.

He rose again as He said He would, and scores of sober, trustworthy eyewitnesses saw Him after His return from among the dead. Better than all, His Spirit now reveals to the Christian heart not a dead Christ but a living one. This we are sent to declare with all the bold dogmatism of those who know, who have been there and experienced it beyond the possibility of a doubt.

The gospel is the official proclamation that Christ died for us and is risen again, with the added announcement that everyone who will believe, and as a result of that belief will cast in his lot with Christ in full and final committal, shall be saved eternally. He must come with the understanding that he will not be popular and that he will be called to stand where Jesus stood before the world: to be admired by many, loved by a few, and rejected at last by the majority of men. He must be willing to pay this price; or let him go his way; Christ has nothing more to say to him now.

The Christian's message to the world must also be one of sin, righteousness, and judgment. He must not accept in any measure the world's moral code, but stand boldly to oppose it and warn of the consequences of following it. And this he must do loudly and persistently, meanwhile taking great care that he himself walk so circumspectly that no flaw may be found in his life to give the lie to his testimony.

There is one thing more: The Christian witness includes also the faithful warning that God is a just and holy Being who will not trifle with men nor allow them to trifle with Him. He is longsuffering and waits patiently to be gracious, but after a while the friendly invitation of the gospel is withdrawn. The effort to persuade the incorrigible sinner is discontinued, death fixes the status of the man who loved his sins and he is sent to the place of the rejected where there is for him no further hope. That is hell, and it may be well we know so little about it. What we do know is sufficiently terrifying.

To His own children God has much more to say, so much that it requires a lifetime of eager listening to hear it all; but His message to the world is simple and brief. It is the work of the church to keep on repeating it to each generation of men till it is either accepted or rejected by those who hear.

The Christian must not allow himself to be entrapped by current vogues in religion, and above all he must never go to the world for his message. He is a man of heaven sent to give witness on earth. As he shall give account to the Lord that bought him, let him see to his commission.

14

THE JOURNEY
OF THE CHURCH

To God's elect, exiles scattered throughout . . .

1 PETER 1:1

This final chapter is intended to be a message of encouragement in a time of political, social, and economic upheaval. In the midst of all the turmoil on earth, there is One walking through the storm. His name is Jesus. He is Christ the Lord. We ought never be frightened—even for a moment—because Jesus is the Sovereign Lord.

The apostle John informs us that after Jesus had fed the multitude, our Lord perceived that the satisfied people "would come and take him by force, to make him a king." So Jesus "departed again into a mountain himself alone" (John 6:15). It is there that we pick up the narrative:

And when even was now come, his disciples went down unto the sea, And entered into a ship, and went over the sea toward Capernaum. And it was now dark, and Jesus was not come to them. And the sea arose by reason of a great wind that blew. So when they had rowed about five and twenty or thirty furlongs, they see Jesus walking on the sea, and drawing nigh unto the ship: and they were afraid. But he saith unto them, It is I; be not afraid. Then they willingly received him into the ship: and immediately the ship was at the land whither they went. (John 6:16–21)

Note the elements of action. Jesus withdraws to the mountain, presumably for reflection and prayer; in the gathering evening darkness, the disciples set out by small ship for Capernaum, their home base. A sudden tempest turns Galilee into an angry sea, and the frightened disciples struggle in their storm-tossed boat. Then they see Jesus walking on the water. Assured that it is He, they take Him into the ship, and, miraculously, they are at their destination.

This episode becomes a prophetic drama of the church as she awaits the return of her Lord and the predestined summation of all things. It was not by coincidence that our Lord went up into the mountain and the disciples went down to the sea. I believe the Lord was giving us a very beautiful object lesson, leading us into thoughts concerning the hope of His return to earth. With all my heart, I believe that Jesus will return soon. I believe He will walk on our troubled sea, just as He walked on the Sea of Galilee to His struggling disciples. Perhaps we think we do not need Him badly enough. When our need here is so great that we can no longer get along without Him, He will come!

AN INSPIRING LORD JESUS

There are some beautiful and inspiring things we should note about the person of the Lord Jesus Christ as we proceed. As I have mentioned, after feeding the five thousand people, Jesus perceived that the gratified, enthusiastic crowd wanted to take Him by force to make Him their King. So He departed again into a mountain alone, the disciples meanwhile going down to the sea to board a small ship that they would sail or row to Capernaum.

Notice first that Jesus declined the offer of the multitude to make Him King. The average man would not have declined a crown, but Jesus Christ is not the average man; He is the Sovereign Lord of the universe. He declined their offer of a crown because He knew the crown they wanted to give Him was not the crown He was destined to wear. Our Lord knew, also, that this was not the right time for a crown. He knew a cross awaited Him before there could be a crown.

We can be assured that our Lord Jesus Christ never did the expected thing, as other men might do. To my mind, He is the supreme Poet and Artist and Musician of all the world. All that is beautiful and lovely and gracious and desirable gather themselves up in our heavenly Bridegroom.

His birth was not a common birth, for our Lord stooped to mortal flesh to be born of the virgin Mary. He has, by the manner of His birth, elevated and dignified human birth beyond all possibilities of description.

The work Jesus did was not common work, even though He humbled Himself to work at the carpenter's bench. What He did was to elevate all labor to an uncommon level and to dignify the most humble toil.

Jesus suffered when He was on earth, and yet His suffering was not the common, tight-lipped, cold-eyed suffering that goes on in our world. It was not the suffering that destroys the higher regions of the spirit and bestializes us, making us like the clay from which we came. The suffering of our Lord was uncommon because everything He did and said rose infinitely above the level of the common.

RAISED ABOVE
THE COMMON LEVEL

If we belong to Jesus now in faith, He has raised us above the level of the common, so that we ourselves as children of God no longer do what is common. It is this elevation of things by the suffering Savior that explains why the most common act becomes an extraordinary act when it is done by the believer in the spirit of Christ's compassion.

Our Lord also stooped to die, but His dying was not the common dying of a man. It was not the discharge of a debt to nature. It was not the final payment on a mortgage held over Him by nature. Nature never held a mortgage on Jesus Christ. He was nature's Creator, not her debtor.

What made Jesus' death uncommon, unusual? It was the dying of the just for the unjust. It was His sacrificial dying, His vicarious dying. He paid a debt He did not owe in behalf of others too deeply in debt ever to pay out.

Being that kind of a Lord in His life and in His death, it is to be expected that His words were never common words. We understand well why His words never will be comprehended by rank-and-file, unconverted men and women. But we understand, too, why His words have always fallen like grace and truth upon the ears of the humble in heart and the meek in spirit.

Has this not been the testimony through the years of all the saints of God? They have come to the Scriptures like bees to flowers, carrying away the sweet and precious nectar for their spiritual needs. But then they have returned again and found that there was still as much nectar as there had been before. Like the Zarephath widow's barrel of meal that was not used up and the jug of oil that did not run dry (1 Kings 17:7–16), every text of Scripture, every word of our Sovereign Lord, yields precious treasures no matter how often we consult it, no matter how acute our need.

So it was with the acts of Jesus. We see it in our Lord's refusal of the crown and His withdrawal to the mountain. If Jesus had stooped to receive the crown they offered, Israel would have rallied behind Him in a moment. But Jesus took the cross in the will of God rather than a crown out of the will of God. What meaning, what direction there is for each of us here!

It takes some of us a long time to learn that the crown before the cross is only worthless tin. It is cheap and gilded, and when we examine it closely we see the inscription "Made in Hell." It is not a crown that came down from heavenly glory but a crown that came from below—a false crown for the person who will take it before he or she takes the cross.

THE WILL OF GOD
IS ALWAYS BEST

At the risk of repeating a religious cliché, I must point out that the will of God is always best, whatever the circumstances. Jesus refused the crown and deliberately took the cross because the cross was in the will of God, both for Him and for humankind.

Let us not be afraid to take that cross ourselves and trust God to provide the crown in His own time. Why should so many in our day try to short-circuit their spiritual lives by eliminating the cross en route to the crown?

Our Lord took the Father's will. He refused the crown that Israel wanted to give Him and instead took the cross the Romans gave Him. On the third day He arose from the dead. Forty days later, He ascended to His Father's right hand, His disciples seeing Him go. And there He is today!

Back to the episode in John 6, what did Jesus do when He was in the mountain alone? He prayed. Jesus, that praying man of all praying men, that example of all praying men, was talking to His heavenly Father. He was talking to Him about the little group of disciples whom He had just parted from a short time before—and about the five thousand people who had just been fed and in their ignorance wanted to make Him their King.

By the human reckoning of the multitude, Jesus would bring about a revolution that would set Israel free, as in the days of Gideon and the great judges and prophets of the Old Testament. But Jesus knew these people well. He knew the worst thing He could do would be to put on a crown and bring that carnal multitude into an earthly kingdom.

Actually, there would have to be many changes among them before they dared become sons and daughters of an earthly kingdom. So He was praying for them in their ignorance and in their confusion, praying to the heavenly Father for His sheep. *And that is exactly what He is doing now!* Jesus is in heaven, praying for His people. I do not mean that our Lord is on His knees continually in the glory land yonder, but He is in continual communion with the Father. "Wherefore he is able also to save them to the uttermost that come unto God by him, seeing he ever liveth to make intercession for them" (Heb. 7:25).

PRAYING WITHOUT CEASING

Years ago, dear old Max Reich, who spoke in our church a number of times, was asked to describe his prayer life. "If you are asking me about getting by myself and spending long periods alone on my knees in prayer, then I would have to say that I am relatively a prayerless man," Dr. Reich told us. "But if you accept praying without ceasing as a continual, humble communion with God, day and night, under all circumstances—the pouring out of my heart to God in continual, unbroken fellowship— then I can say I pray without ceasing."

I believe this is the manner in which our Lord is remembering us at the Father's throne. His communion with the Father speaks to us of the necessity of a continual communion of our souls with God. This kind of communion and devotion does not consist of words.

I once wrote an editorial that I titled "Wordless Worship." In it I tried to present the idea that there is a worship that goes beyond human words. In fact, I have come to the conclusion that whatever can be put into words is second rate, for there are divine spiritualities that cannot be expressed.

In fact, Paul called these divine spiritualities "inexpressible." They are the eternal things that do not pass away. It is here that we need to remember that God is allowing us to live at the same time on two planes. He permits us to live on the religious plane, where there are preachers and song leaders and choirs and organists and pianists and editors and leaders and promoters and evangelists. That is religion. That is religion in overalls—the external garb of religion. It has its place in God's work and plan. But beyond and superior to all of the externals in our religious experience is the spiritual essence of it all. And it is that spiritual essence for which I plead. I long to see it enthroned in our communion and fellowship in the church of Jesus Christ.

We have many Bible conferences that begin and end in themselves. They circle fully around themselves, and after the benediction everyone goes home no better than he or she was before. That is the woe and the terror of these conferences. I plead for something more than textualism that begins and ends with itself and sees nothing beyond.

WE MUST PRESS ON IN THE HOLY SPIRIT

If we do not see beyond the visible, if we cannot touch that which is intangible, if we cannot hear that which is inaudible, if we cannot know that which is beyond knowing, then I have serious doubts about the validity of our Christian experience. The Bible tells us, "Eye hath not seen, nor ear heard, neither have entered into the heart of man, the things which God hath prepared for them that love him" (1 Cor. 2:9).

That is why Paul goes on to remind us that God has revealed these mysteries to us by the Holy Spirit. If we would only stop trying to make the Holy Spirit our servant and begin to live in Him as the fish lives in the sea, we would enter into the riches of glory about which we know nothing now.

Too many want the Holy Spirit in order that they may have the gift of healing. Others want Him for the gift of tongues. Still others seek Him so that their testimony may become effective. All of these things, I will grant, are a part of the total pattern of the New Testament. But it is impossible for us to make God our servant. Let us never pray that we may be filled with the Spirit of God for secondary purposes. God wants to fill us with His Spirit in order that we should know Him first of all and be absorbed in Him. We should enter into the fullness of the Spirit so that God's Son may be glorified in us.

I try to bathe my soul in the writings and the hymns of the devoted saints of God who lived centuries ago. These were men and women who walked with God, then were no more because God took them to Himself. They left behind such themes as "Jesus, Thou Joy of Loving Hearts" and "Jesus, the Very Thought of Thee with Sweetness Fills My Breast." When I sense the shining glory of the life and works of these choice saints of the past, I wonder why we ever stoop to read or sing or quote anything but that which is elevated and divine, noble and inspiring.

JESUS PRAYS FOR US

Jesus declined the crown. Instead, He went up into the mountain. His presence there actually is prayer. At the Father's throne He is not everlastingly naming His people in pleadings and petitions. He is not talking on and on, as some of us do, covering our inward fears by our multitude of words. No, it is His presence at the right hand of the Father that constitutes His intercession for us. The fact that He is there is the might of His prayer, and that prayer is for His people—for you and me and for the whole church of Jesus Christ.

In this Galilean drama, it is not difficult to envision the Christian church. As it is told in the first two chapters of the Acts, Jesus had not more than reached the heavenly mountain when suddenly the disciples were filled with the Holy Spirit and the church of Christ was launched on the sea, on the dark sea. And she has been on that sea ever since.

When our Lord went up into the mountain and the clouds received Him out of their sight, the Light of the world went away, and night came. Jesus had warned His disciples, "Yet a little while is the light with you. Walk while ye have the light, lest darkness come upon you" (John 12:35).

It is altogether true that night has settled on the world, and the church has worked in darkness through the years. I do not mean that the church has had no light, but I do say that the condition of the world has been darkness, and it has been as night upon the world throughout these centuries. The Dark Ages in history rightly should take in all of the time since the Sun of Righteousness withdrew His physical presence, for it has been dark all over the world since He left the earth.

The disciples were on the sea. The sea can be very inviting and yet very unpredictable and treacherous. It can be calm today and violent tomorrow. The sea bears its cargoes in peace and tranquility today, but tomorrow it will dash them into the murky depths. For the disciples that night, Galilee was a contrary, troubled, restless sea—disturbed, turbulent, treacherous, cruel, potentially deadly.

In the Scriptures, the world of humanity is sometimes metaphorically referred to as the sea. Indeed, humankind is not unlike the sea I have just described. The leaders of the nations meet at conference tables, shake hands, and toast one another. They have their pictures taken together. Outwardly they laugh and joke as if in friendship. But the next day these men are enemies again, and they would kill each other if given a chance. We live in a turbulent, cruel, treacherous world.

CONTACT WITHOUT MERGING

Even the relationship of the ship to the sea is illustrative. It was a relationship of contact without merging. That ought to be the relation of the church to the world. The world is real, and the Christian church is here in this world for a purpose. Thank God, we are on top of the "sea." We maintain the same relation to the world as did that little ship to the Sea of Galilee. It is contact without merging.

Our problem is the same one the disciples faced. The sea is always trying to get into the ship—the world is always trying to get into the church. The world around us continues to try to find its way in, to splash in, to come in with soft words and beautiful white crests, forever whispering, "Don't be so aloof; don't be so hostile. Let me come in. I have something for you—something that will do you good!" The world is making offers to the church, but the church does not need the world! The world has nothing that the Christian church needs.

Granted, there is the sense of need we have because we are human beings and citizens. I get my food through the efforts of farmers and ranchers, I travel the highways of our nation, I depend upon police and firemen. And so do you. But that is another thing altogether. Even in those matters, we are not merging; we are in contact without merging.

Some people say they are helped in their faith through the offerings of science and the answers of education. I have a little book in my study (I use it for a window prop when I want to get more air) that has chapters entitled, "Finding God through Science," "Finding God through Nature," "Finding God through Art." Why should we be trying to find God through a back door? Why should we always be peering out of some cellar window looking for God when the whole top side of the building is made of sheer crystal and God is shining down—revealed? We need to open the skylights of our hearts, look up, and invite God in.

I am sure the disciples were busy bailing on that wildly stormy night, trying to keep the water out of their boat. It was a question of survival. And, whether we believe it or not, it is a question of survival with the church of Jesus Christ today! It is not enough to lean back on our forebears and say with the first-century Jews, "We have Abraham to our father." John the Baptist told them, "And now also the axe is laid unto the root of the trees: therefore every tree which bringeth not forth good fruit is hewn down, and cast into the fire" (Matt. 3:9–10).

DENOMINATIONS DO NOT COUNT

The living God is not worried about our denominations and our churchly traditions. He is not pledged to preserve our religious family trees. He only wants to get the world evangelized. God is not concerned about preserving any of our Christian denominations, but He is concerned about the life of the church of Jesus Christ—the spiritual church, regardless of what she may call herself. Our Lord is concerned that the church of Jesus Christ should be saved from the incoming waves. A little of the world here, a little there—these move in on the church until the time comes when we no longer have a spiritual church. Instead, we have a sinking vessel.

For the disciples in the boat, their intention was to cross to Capernaum. For them, Capernaum was home. The disciples were in the ship on their way home, and it was night. In our day, the church of Jesus Christ is on her way home, still toiling, still rowing, and it is night.

When we think about the church, the real church of Jesus Christ, some of us hold such an ideal picture in our minds that it is hard to be realistic about the toiling and the rowing. We think of the church in idealistic terms—fixed up and garnished and made beautiful in all ways.

But those disciples in the boat were not idealists; they were realists. They smelled of the sea. Their language was not schooled and academic. They were plain men who were sailing home.

Their situation was not a perfect one and their talk was not necessarily about sacred themes. They may have argued. One or two may have sulked. Someone perhaps went to sleep and did not pull his weight. But they were all sailing home together, and Jesus was on the mountain praying for them all.

So it is today in the church of Jesus Christ. There are still disagreements among the people of God. There were in Paul's day, and there are now. There are many imperfections among us. There are existing conditions that ought not to be there—but they are. On the sea that night long ago, the disciples were tired, weary, sleepy, homesick—sailing for Capernaum and home. Their situation was not ideal. They were still in human circumstances. But they were the apple of our Lord's eye. He loved them, and He prayed for them.

WE AWAIT JESUS' RETURN

"And it was now dark," the Scriptures say, "and Jesus was not come to them" (John 6:17). For the church of Jesus Christ, it was dark in the first and second centuries, and Jesus did not come. It was dark in the days of Constantine, it was dark when Bernard of Clairvaux lived, it was dark when Martin Luther preached. It was dark when John Wesley stood on the tombstone to preach, it was dark when George Fox walked the hills and vales of England. And in all that time Jesus did not come. It is *still* dark, and we still wait. We do not want to admit that we are disappointed, but we are, nevertheless!

As the wind rose and the tempest in its fury tossed their ship, no doubt the disciples on the Sea of Galilee cried out, "Where are You, Lord?" And the church of Jesus Christ, caught in a moral tempest that threatens to tear it apart, makes the same plea. Thank God, we have Christ's assurance that "the gates of hell shall not prevail against" His church (Matt. 16:18). Churches may die, but the church still lives. The church of Jesus Christ, composed of all the people of God, shall never perish!

I remind you that Jesus Christ is still Lord. He is still the head of His body, the church. We do not have to apologize for Him. He does not want us to soften His gospel to make it more acceptable to the world. He is not looking for us to defend Him, to argue on His behalf. His eyes see through the darkness. He holds the church in the hollow of His hand even while it is being tossed on the wild sea.

And just as He left the mountain at the proper time, miraculously walking on the water to join His struggling disciples, so He will return from heaven to gather us up and bring us home. He is not here yet, but He is coming! We do not know when He will come within hailing distance, but we know He will come at just the right time. His love and His keen interest in His people will not permit Him to remain away longer than necessary.

Let us not be fearful. The Savior is walking on the sea. He is coming our way. Though it is dark and the winds blow strong, our little ship is on its way Home!

REFERENCES

Chapter 1: The Necessity of the Church

God Tells the Man Who Cares: God Speaks to Those Who Take Time to Listen, compiled by Anita M. Bailey (Chicago: Moody Publishers, 1993), 22–24.

Chapter 2: The Lord of the Church

God Tells the Man Who Cares, 185–194.

Chapter 3: The Spirit of the Church

God's Pursuit of Man (Camp Hill, PA: Christian Publications, 1950; repr. Chicago, IL: Moody Publishers, 2015), 91–99.

Chapter 4: The Organization of the Church

"Set in Order the Things That Are Wanting," sermon preached on February 16, 1958.

Chapter 5: The Leadership of the Church

"Qualifications for Church Leadership," Parts 1 and 2, sermons preached on February 23 and March 2, 1958.

Chapter 6: The Character of the Church

The Counselor (Chicago: Moody Publishers, 2015), 10–24.

Chapter 7: The Unity of the Church

The Counselor, 114–116; *God Tells the Man Who Cares*, 45–48.

Chapter 8: The Communion of the Church

Man, The Dwelling Place of God; What It Means to Have Christ Living in You, compiled by Anita M. Bailey (Chicago: WingSpread Publishers, 2008), 78–86.

Chapter 9: The Freedom of the Church

"The Church's Lack of Freedom: Four Stages on the Path Toward Spiritual Perfection," sermon preached on March 24, 1957.

Chapter 10: The Ability of the Church

The Counselor, 116–130.

Chapter 11: The Purpose of the Church

The Best of A. W. Tozer, Book One, compiled by Warren Wiersbe (Chicago: Moody Publishers, 2000), 217–222.

Chapter 12: The Service of the Church

"Serving Members Make a Serving Church: Life of the Servant," sermon preached on February 1, 1959.

Chapter 13: The Witness of the Church

God Tells the Man Who Cares, 32–39.

Chapter 14: The Journey of the Church

Faith Beyond Reason (Camp Hill, PA: Christian Publications, Inc.; repr., Chicago: WingSpread Publishers, 2009), 145–160.

ENCOUNTER GOD. WORSHIP MORE.

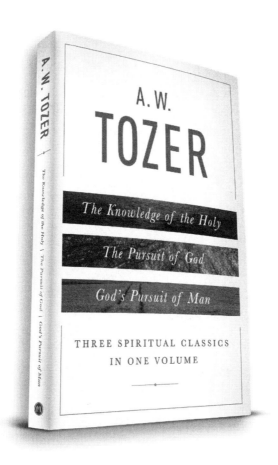

STUDY THE BIBLE WITH PROFESSORS FROM MOODY BIBLE INSTITUTE

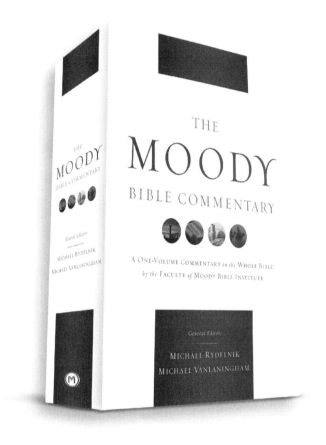

MOODY Publishers

*From the Word **to** Life*

Study the Bible with a team of 30 Moody Bible Institute professors. This in-depth, user-friendly, one-volume commentary will help you better understand and apply God's Word to all of life. Additional study helps include maps, charts, bibliographies for further reading, and a subject and Scripture index.

978-0-8024-2867-7　|　also available as an eBook

THE SPIRITUAL JOURNEY OF A. W. TOZER

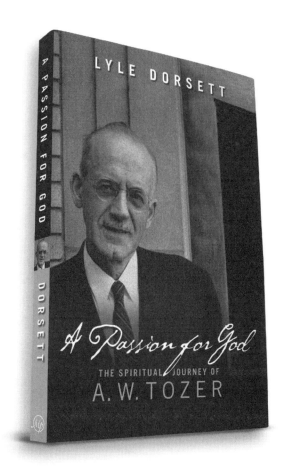